# Jordan

The Contemporary Middle East

Edited by
**Professor Anoushiravan Ehteshami**
Centre for Middle Eastern and Islamic Studies,
University of Durham, UK

For well over a century now the Middle East and North African countries have formed a central plank of the international system. **The Contemporary Middle East** series provides the first systematic attempt at studying the key actors of this dynamic, complex, and strategically important region. Using an innovative common format – which in each case study provides an easily-digestible analysis of the origins of the state, its contemporary politics, economics and international relations – prominent Middle East experts have been brought together to write definitive studies of the MENA region's key countries.

**Books in the series**

Jordan: A Hashemite legacy
*Beverley Milton-Edwards and Peter Hinchcliffe*

Syria: Revolution from above
*Raymond Hinnebusch*

# Jordan

## A HASHEMITE LEGACY

Beverley Milton-Edwards
and
Peter Hinchcliffe

London and New York

First published 2001
by Routledge
11 New Fetter Lane, London EC4P 4EE

Simultaneously published in the USA and Canada
by Routledge
29 West 35th Street, New York, NY 10001

*Routledge is an imprint of the Taylor & Francis Group*

Typeset by Expo Holdings, Malaysia
Printed and bound in Great Britain by MPG Books Ltd, Bodmin

**British Library Cataloguing in Publication Data**

A catalogue record for this book is available from the British Library.

ISBN: 0–415–26726–9

# TABLE OF CONTENTS

# CHRONOLOGY

**BC**

| | |
|---|---|
| c2000 | Amorites destroyed urban culture and eventually established Canaan (modern Palestine, Jordan and Syria) |
| c1482 | Canaan under control of Pharaoh Tuthmosis III |
| c1250 | Start of 'biblical period' Israelites under Moses pass through 'Jordan' |
| c1200–332 | Iron Age. Development and consolidation of three kingdoms of Edom (south of the Dead Sea), Moab (central Jordan) and Ammon – north |
| 961–922 | King Solomon's rule included lands east of the river Jordan |
| 587 | King Nebuchadnezzar II of Babylon destroys Jerusalem |
| c500 | Nabataeans made Petra their capital |
| 332 | Brief Hellenistic period following conquest of Persia by Alexander the Great and extension of his empire |
| 301–198 | Ptolemies in control |
| 198–63 | Seleucids (based in Damascus) rule |

**AD**

| | |
|---|---|
| 63BC–324 AD | Period of Roman rule (AD 105/6 Petra incorporated into Roman Empire) |
| 632 | Death of the Prophet Mohammed followed by Muslim conquests |
| 661 | Damascus declared capital of Ummayyad Empire |
| 750 | Abbasids overthrow Ummayyads. Capital moved to Baghdad |
| 1071 | Seljuk Turks seize Baghdad |
| 1099 | First Crusade capture of Jerusalem. Later establishment of Outre Jourdain by Crusaders |
| 1174 | Salah al Din (Saladin) seized power as Sultan of Egypt. Ayyubid dynasty |
| 1187 | Decisive victory over Crusaders by Saladin followed by recapture of Jerusalem |
| 1260 | Mamluks overthrow Ayyubids |
| 1517 | Ottoman Sultan Selim I captures Mamluk Egypt and its dependencies. Period of stagnation in Ottoman controlled Jordan |
| 1897 | First Zionist Congress (at Basle). Creation of Zionist Organisation with aim to establish a home in Palestine for 'the Jewish People' |
| 1900–08 | Construction of Hijaz Railway linking Damascus and Medina |
| 1914 | Outbreak of First World War. Ottoman Empire sides with Germany |
| 1915 | Hussein-McMahon correspondence and Sykes-Picot agreement. Conflicting undertakings with regard to the shape of post-war Middle East |
| 1916 | Arab revolt under leadership of Sherif Hussein of Mecca |
| 1917 | Balfour Declaration promising British support for a 'national home for the Jewish people in Palestine' |
| 1918 | Amir Faisal bin Hussein leads Arab forces into Damascus |
| 1919 | Post-war Versailles conference. Faisal presses for Arab autonomy |
| 1920 | San Remo conference endorses division of much of the Middle East between Britain and France. Britain awarded mandate for Palestine including East Bank |
| 1921 | Cairo conference sub-divides 'Palestine'. Abdullah bin Hussein appointed Amir of Transjordan |

| | |
|---|---|
| 1922 | League of Nations exempts Transjordan from provisions of the Mandate for Palestine |
| 1923 | Britain recognises Transjordan as a national state being prepared for independence |
| 1928 | Anglo-Transjordanian Treaty provides for wide measure of self-government |
| April 1928 | Promulgation of Transjordan Organic Law (Constitution) |
| 1936 | Arab revolt in Palestine |
| 1937 | Peel Commission proposes Arab part of Palestine be joined to Transjordan |
| 1939 | Outbreak of Second World War |
| 1941 | Arab Legion participates in Iraqi and Syrian campaigns |
| 1945 | Transjordan founder member of League of Arab States |
| 1946 | Treaty of London. Independence of Transjordan as a Kingdom. Amir Abdullah proclaimed King Abdullah I |
| 1947 | UN recommends partition of Palestine |
| 1948 | First Arab-Israeli war. Arab Legion successfully defends Arab East Jerusalem |
| 1949 | King Abdullah annexes territory held by his forces on the West Bank. Kingdom renamed 'Hashemite Kingdom of Jordan' |
| 1951 | King Abdullah assassinated in Jerusalem. Son Talal becomes King |
| 1952 | New Constitution promulgated (still largely in force) |
| August 1952 | King Talal abdicates. Son Hussein proclaimed King |
| 1955 | Intense popular opposition to prospect of Jordan joining Baghdad Pact |
| 1956 | King Hussein dismisses General Glubb and other British officers in Arab Legion. General election on a multi-party basis returns radical government headed by Suleiman Nablusi |
| 1957 | Anglo-Jordanian agreement abrogated Anglo-Jordanian treaty of 1946. Removal of remaining British troops and military installations. King Hussein defeats attempted coup by Lt.Col. Ali Abu Nowar |
| 1958 | Merger of Kingdoms of Iraq and Jordan: Arab Federation |
| July 1958 | Hashemite Monarchy in Baghdad overthrown. British troops flown to Jordan at request of King Hussein |
| 1960 | Assassination of Jordanian Prime Minister Hazza al Majali |
| 1964 | Cairo Arab summit primarily to discuss Jordan water problem. United Arab military command established under Egyptian leadership |
| December 1964 | Al Fatah founded as activist wing of PLO under Arafat's leadership. Al Fatah attacks on Israel from Jordanian and Lebanese territory |
| 1966 | Israeli army destroys West Bank town of As Samu in retaliation for guerrilla attacks |
| 1967 | 'June War': Jordan loses all territory on the West Bank including Arab East Jerusalem. 200,000 refugees flee from West Bank to Jordan |
| August 1967 | Khartoum Arab summit approves subsidies to 'front line states' including Jordan |
| November 1967 | UN Security Council adopts Resolution no. 242 |
| 1968 | Battle of Karameh. Jordanian Army and PLO fighters repulse attack by Israeli armoured unit. Increasing confrontation (1968 and 1969) between PLO and Jordanian Government |
| 1970 | 'Black September' marks start of civil war. Jordanian regime versus Palestinian guerrillas |

| | |
|---|---|
| 1971 | Jordanian army completes defeat of Palestinian groups. PLO leadership expelled |
| 1972 | King Hussein state visit to US. American pledges of increased economic and military support |
| 1973 | Third Arab-Israeli war. Jordanian forces do not participate. Security Council Resolution 338 reiterated 'Land for Peace' formula as stated in SCR 242 |
| 1974 | Rabat Arab summit recognises PLO as 'only legitimate representative of the Palestinian people'. House of Representatives dissolved. King ruling by decree |
| 1978 | Camp David peace agreement between Egypt and Israel. Jordan joins with other Arab countries in rejecting it and imposing sanctions on Cairo |
| | 60 member National Consultative Council (NCC) established |
| 1982 | Israeli invasion of Lebanon. Jordan is the key participant in President Reagan's peace initiative involving proposed association between Jordan and an autonomous Palestinian entity on the West Bank |
| 1984 | Jordan re-establishes diplomatic relations with Egypt |
| 1985 | Joint Jordanian/Palestinian peace proposals in context of future Jordanian/Palestinian confederation |
| 1987 | Palestinian 'Intifada' (uprising) breaks out |
| 1988 | Jordan formally breaks links with West Bank. King Hussein accepts that Jordan can not realistically purport to represent the interests of the Palestinians |
| 1989 | Widespread riots and demonstrations sparked off by removal of subsidies on fuel. King dismisses government of Zaid Rifai |
| April 1989 | Emergency IMF/IBRD programme to rescue the Jordanian economy. First General Election since 1967. Moslem Brotherhood candidates win 20 seats and other Islamic bloc candidates 14 |
| 1990 | Royal Commission appointed to draft National Charter to liberalise and regulate political life in Jordan |
| August 1990 | Iraqi invasion of Kuwait. Jordan populace strongly supportive of Saddam Hussein. Jordan refuses to align itself with US led 'Desert Storm' coalition |
| 1991 | Liberation of Kuwait. Temporary cooling of relations between Jordan and the West plus many Arab states. Influx of refugees into Jordan from the Gulf – mostly Jordanian/Palestinians reach 350,000 |
| June 1991 | National Charter endorsed by King |
| July 1991 | King Hussein repeals martial law in force since 1967 |
| October 1991 | Opening of the Madrid Peace Conference. Jordan acts as 'umbrella' for Palestinian delegation |
| 1992 | House of Representatives adopts legislation legalising political parties |
| 1993 | Oslo Agreement: 'Declaration of Principles' agreed after secret talks between Israeli and Palestinian negotiators. Jordan and Israel conclude 'common agenda' for subsequent bilateral negotiations |
| November 1993 | General election for National Assembly. Islamic Action Front (IAF) win 16 seats and independents 45 (out of 80) |
| 1994 | Intensive peace negotiations with Israel. Washington Declaration (July) ends state of war. Full Peace Treaty signed in October. National Assembly approves legislation for municipal elections in Amman |

| | |
|---|---|
| 1995 | Confrontational policy towards Iraq following defection to Jordan of Saddam Hussein's two son-in laws. King Hussein authorises Iraqi opposition movement (Iraqi National Accord) to open HQ in Amman |
| November 1995 | Assassination of Israeli Prime Minister Yitzhak Rabin. King Hussein attends the funeral in Jerusalem. |
| 1996 | Municipal elections. Islamic and left wing groups fail to get support King Hussein pays official visit to TelAviv. Number of bilateral agreements signed |
| August 1996 | Food riots following removal of subsidies on bread and other food-stuffs. King Hussein's new posture towards Baghdad leads to reconciliation with Saudi Arabia |
| 1997 | Right wing coalition government headed by Mr Netanyahu comes to power in Israel. Middle East Peace Process (MEPP) stagnates. Attempted assassination of Islamic radical leader in Amman by Israeli agents leads to crisis in relations with Israel |
| November 1997 | General Elections boycotted by Islamic parties on grounds that amended electoral law is loaded against them. Also protest at draconian press laws |
| 1998 | King Hussein spends last four months of the year under treatment for cancer in United States. Crown Prince Hassan regent |
| 1999 | King Hussein returns to Amman terminally ill. Dismisses Hassan as Crown Prince and appoints eldest son Abdullah in his place. Dies a week later |
| February 1999 | Abdullah proclaimed as King Abdullah II. Half brother Hamza appointed Crown Prince. New Government (with old faces) appointed |
| March 1999 | King Abdullah starts a series of regional and international visits to seek financial support and to heal wounds opened by his father |
| June 1999 | Local government elections including participation by Islamic parties who poll well |
| November 1999 | Hamas leadership exiled and offices closed in Amman |

# PREFACE

The purpose of this book is to provide an introduction and overview of modern-day Jordan and in the five chapters we will introduce a number of major points and issues which have characterised this state. This book has been written with the non-specialist reader in mind. The themes discussed in this book have been identified as essential to any understanding of this small but pivotal kingdom and the immense pressures on internal politics that external factors have always played. By this we mean to highlight, from the very start, that the emergence of Jordan as a modern nation–state was not the product of some slow evolutionary process but rather the result of colonial amibtion in the Middle East. In this sense Jordan, or Transjordan as it was first known, was an artifical creation designed as a cheap sop to Arab nationalist ambition envisioned by the Hashemites of the Hijaz.

From such paltry beginnings, however, the Hashemites, under King Abdullah and then his grandson King Hussein, carved out a nation state whose future as now been assured with the smooth succession of Hussein's son Abdullah II in February 1999. The five main chapters of this book will examine dimensions of Jordan which remain pertinent to understanding the processes of nation creation and state-building which emerged in this land. For not only were the Hashemites faced with the formidable task of state-building and the accompanying economic development, but they were also compelled to create a sense of nation among a disparate group of peoples. The keys to these processes are revealed in the chapters which focus on the country's political developments from the First World War to the end of the twentieth century.

The chapter on the Jordanian economy reveals the dependent-nature of this particular country on factors outside its own borders. It also highlights the vulnerability of this particular economy to issues of migrant labour, economic structural adjustment programmes and aid debt-dependency. The dependent nature of Jordan's political system and its vulnerability to external regional factors is also revealed in the chapter on international relations. The primary focus here is the regional context and the contradictory pulls and pushes which Jordan has experienced from its near neighbours including Syria, Israel, Iraq and Saudi Arabia. The territorial ambitions of Jordan's own leadership is also examined revealing fresh insights into power politics in the Middle East region.

This book, then is a fresh insight on contemporary Jordan and its future status in the Middle East region. It is designed to assist new readers to the subject in understanding the complex interplay of politics, economy and international relations upon the future of this tiny yet significant state. While Jordan may no longer enjoy the diplomatic importance it garnered under King Hussein, its place in the regiona, order has an assured future.

The list of those who we would like to thank includes our many friends in Jordan who have assisted with the preparation of this book but who, for political reasons, cannot be mentioned. Without their dilligent assistance this book would not have been possible. We would also like to extend our thanks to Series Editor Anoush Ehteshami for his encouragement and everyone at Harwood Academic Publishers involved in its production. Our gratitude is also extended to colleagues and friends at Queen's University of Belfast, School of Politics and Edinburgh University, Centre for the Advanced Study of Islam and the Middle East. We would also like to express our appreciation to Jane Taylor for the cover photo. Final thanks to Graham and Archie, our supportive partners and fellow travellers.

# INTRODUCTION

This book focuses on the Hashemite Kingdom of Jordan as part of a series on the main countries within the Middle East and North Africa (MENA) region. It is intended for a general reader, who is not necessarily a specialist, but one who has some familiarity with the main issues facing the area. The publication is intended to be a brief but comprehensive guide to Jordan and one which will suggest further reading for a more in depth study of the Hashemite Kingdom.

This volume on Jordan employs a common format to its companions in the Contemporary Middle East series. Following the introduction the book will examine the country under five headings: (A) State formation covering the historical background to the creation of modern Jordan in 1922 and its subsequent history up to the assassination of King Abdullah I in 1952. (B) Contemporary politics including the development of political life under the reign of King Hussein and contemporary pressures for democratisation. (C) The economy and its effect on the Kingdom's policies. (D) International relations and finally (E) – Whither Jordan? – an assessment of the current political and economic climate of the country and its position within the region in the new millennium.

Jordan lies in the heartland of the Arab world. It is both geographically and demographically small, making it a weak country with limited natural resources. Yet as a front line party in the Arab-Israeli conflict and as what has often been described as a pivotal state its perceived importance as a regional player is out of all proportion to its intrinsic size and power. Jordan does, in a phrase ascribed to a former British foreign minister, 'box above her weight'.

Much of the Kingdom's importance is also due to geography. Recent history and a number of demographic factors have complicated its fortuitous location, the most important being that it has the longest border with the State of Israel of any Arab country. For nearly 19 years what is now known as the 'West Bank', including east, or 'Arab' Jerusalem, was part of the Kingdom, formally annexed in 1952 as a result of the first (1948) Arab-Israeli war and lost, after less than a week's fighting in the second in June 1967. Proximity to Israel, and Jordan's rule over the West Bank from 1948 to 1967, made it the natural and unavoidable destination for hundreds of thousands of Palestinian refugees in two great exoduses. The first, amounting to a large proportion of the 800,000 who fled their homes in 1948 as large areas of what became Israel were ethnically cleansed during and immediately after the war, and the second in 1967 when many of the original refugees as well as longer term inhabitants of Jordanian-ruled Palestine were once again displaced and sought refuge across the Jordan river. This wave perhaps amounted to as many as 250,000 in June–July 1967 (one quarter of the Palestinians formerly under Jordanian rule on the West Bank), swelling the ranks of the 300,000 dispossessed Palestinians already in TransJordan. It was principally from that moment as Nevo and Pappé put it, that "unlike any other state in the region, in Jordan the Arab-Israeli conflict is both a domestic and a foreign policy issue at the same time" (Nevo and Pappé, 1994, p. 1). In 1967 Jordan lost most of its control and political power over Palestinian land absorbed in 1948 but nevertheless gained a large Palestinian community in refuge east of the river, the great majority of whom, naturally enough, were more concerned with regaining their birthright than with making a contribution to their country of exile.

The instinctive ambivalence of TransJordanians towards their Palestinian guests and in reverse, Palestinian ambivalence towards their hosts and their temporarily adopted King is the great fault line in Jordanian society, a line, however, increasingly blurred by the fact that (as explained in Chapter 1) a significant number of families of Palestinian origin have been in Jordan as long as and in some cases longer than some of their 'true' TransJordanian neighbours. A more widespread cause of national imprecision is inter-marriage. There can be very few Jordanian families, especially in the main urban centres, that do not have Palestinian in-laws. Only one third of the 1.36 million Palestinian refugees registered with the United Nations Relief and Works Agency (UNRWA) living in Jordan (41 per cent of the total refugee population) are still in 'camps' (small houses in townships). The rest are integrated, at a variety of economic and social levels, into Jordanian society, admittedly some in places in identifiable urban areas – virtual ghettos but with others living cheek and jowl with Jordanian neighbours. Palestinians, especially Christian Palestinians, control large parts of the private sector and are prominent throughout the professions. Only the highest ranks in the security and defence establishment are beyond Palestinian reach. In addition they remain numerically under-represented in the higher echelons of government, but have provided Prime Ministers and continue to be represented at ministerial rank (although this is generally by scions of the so-called notable families rather than from the ranks of the 1948 and 1967 refugees).

Since the Palestinian-Jordanian civil conflict between 1970–71 following the forcible expulsion from Jordan of the Palestinian political leadership and its more radical adherents, the Palestinian community has been generally quiescent and outwardly loyal to its adopted country. A significant proportion of them however continue to regard this adoption as a temporary status, especially many of the 400,000 or so still living in camps on the East Bank. This is despite the fact that hope of either returning to their original homes or making a new start in a viable Palestinian state becomes increasingly faint as time goes on. Their loyalty has been tested, especially at times when radical Arabs perceive Jordanian policies as too conciliatory towards Israel or as serving a western (perceived to be United States) agenda rather than an Arab one.

But even following the Jordanian-Israeli Peace Treaty of 1994 and as the Middle East Peace Process (MEPP) became increasingly bogged down, the Palestinians did not take to the streets. To the surprise of some observers they exhibited a much less overt rejectionist stance towards warmer Jordanian ties than many of their home grown TransJordanian neighbours. In this the Palestinians living in Jordan were mainly reflecting a grudging acceptance of a policy of positive engagement with Israel, symbolised by the PLO-Israel Oslo accords of September 1993. Nevertheless, however quiescent the Palestinian community may appear and however integrated into Jordanian society it seems to be, the Jordanian government has constantly to be sensitive to possible reactions to its regional policies by a majority of the population within its borders, hence the regime's traditional and seemingly contradictory policies. On one hand, there are manifestations of pro-Western tendencies as expected of a conservative Arab monarchy and on the other, the periodic striking of radical attitudes more in keeping with its geographical position as a front line state in permanent confrontation with the 'Zionist enemy'. Accordingly the Oslo Accords and the peace treaty with Israel has narrowed Jordan's room for manoeuvre and the total collapse of the MEPP would put considerable pressure on Jordan to re-examine its relationship with Israel. We look at this possibility, amongst others, in the concluding chapter.

There are other factors which contribute to the inflated importance of Jordan as a regional player. Most significantly in recent years has been the personality and longevity of King Hussein who was on the throne from 1952 until early 1999. Throughout the bulk of that period many observers regarded King Hussein as Jordan. In common with other countries in the region – for example 'Assad's Syria' or 'Saddam's Iraq' – the image of the country is subsumed into the personality of the current ruler. Perhaps until his death this applied more so in the case of Jordan as the King had been around for so long. He was a well-known international personality. In the western media – particularly in the United States and Britain – he was often portrayed as a heroic figure: 'The Plucky Little King' as one British tabloid described him early in his reign. Courageous and enduring were the qualities commonly ascribed to him in the West. He was certainly a survivor, as is the Hashemite regime he headed. As Peter Mansfield wrote: "Many obituaries of the Hashemite Kingdom of Jordan have been prepared for instant use. There have been many occasions in the past 40 years when the external and internal forces gathered against this last of the Anglo-Arab monarchies were so strong and numerous that its survival seemed impossible. But it still lives and the obituaries gather on its files" (Mansfield, 1990, p. 417).

The obituaries have now of course appeared. Their effusive sentiments give the lie to those close observers of the Arab world in the late 1950s and throughout the 1960s, including Western ambassadors serving in Amman who were amongst those frequently predicting the imminent demise of the Hashemite monarchy. Jordan on occasions seemed doomed to share the fate of other former Arab kingdoms outside the Arabian peninsular – Egypt in 1952, Tunisia in 1957, Iraq in 1958 (the Baghdad Hashemite branch) and Libya in 1969. But as this book describes the King, over the years, legitimised and entrenched his authority and his position within the Kingdom and became virtually unassailable. The smooth succession of his hastily nominated last minute heir – Abdullah II – is an eloquent testimony to the late King's achievement in securing the position of the monarchy, but presumably (with the removal of his brother Hassan who served as crown prince for over 30 years) only under whom he perceived to be the right monarch. It will be interesting to see what other 'personality regimes' in the region apart from Hashemite Jordan will survive the demise of their current reigning head of state. ('Republican' presidents Assad and Saddam have also striven to create family dynasties to seek the survival of the Alawite and Takriti succession.) In complete contrast to 30 years ago Jordan, even now under a new inexperienced King, is regarded as an oasis of stability in a troubled region. This we should see as something of a (preliminary) vote of confidence in the institution as well as the incumbent.

King Hussein was partly a product of Western education – his experiences at Harrow School in England and as an officer cadet at Sandhurst Military Academy left their mark. His English was perfect; he and his brother, the heir apparent for so long, Hassan, had an extensive network of senior and influential contacts in the West. In the King's case this had been built up over nearly 50 years. Younger Hashemites, including the present King Abdullah II, many of whom have also been educated in Europe and the United States, were encouraged to do likewise. Over time King Hussein became a credible 'Royal' in more of a Western than an oriental mode, in contrast to other Arab traditional rulers of Saudi Arabia or the Gulf States. Perhaps because of the circumstances of Jordan's creation, plus the influence of his beloved grandfather King Abdullah and his own feelings with regard to where his country's best interests lie, he instinctively tended to align himself with the West in the game of nations. But as this book describes he was not always able to do this. He was careful when his survival was at stake to bend to the pressures of Pan-Arabism or Arab nationalism, even when he believed that his or Jordan's interests might suffer. Jordan's disastrous involvement in the 1967 war is a case in point. But he could hardly have kept out of it, so strong was popular enthusiasm throughout the Arab world whipped up by President Nasser of Egypt to join forces with the Egyptians and Syrians to settle with Israel once and for all. As a result he lost half his kingdom. For similar, if more narrowly-based reasons, in 1990–91 he refused to be drawn into the Desert Storm coalition against Saddam Hussein, thus jeopardising his traditional relationship with the West and with his conservative Arab colleagues on whose financial support he relied. But on the whole his balancing act was sure footed, ensuring his position in the region, his own survival (until cancer took him, rather than a bullet) and that of his regime. King Abdullah's II skills remain largely untested, but at least the omens are more propitious than they were when his father came to the throne.

Jordan, even when boxing above its weight, has never been an Arab power of the first rank. Nor has it harboured pretensions to be one. After its annexation of the West Bank it has had no further territorial ambitions. King Abdullah I's dreams of a Hashemite dominated Greater Syria died with him. The short-lived constitutional unity between the Hashemite Kingdoms of Iraq and Jordan was one of a number of unsuccessful similar ventures – Egypt and Syria, Libya and Egypt – inspired by the concept of Pan-Arabism and not in Jordan's case for the sake of territorial aggrandisement. As the chapter on Jordan's international relationships describes, King Hussein skilfully not only manoeuvred between East and West (ensuring his true sympathies were understood where they really mattered) but also chartered a careful course between regional antagonists. He always sought to avoid isolation by attaching himself to one of the centres of power within the shifting sands of Arab power politics, now with Cairo, then with Damascus, usually with an eye cocked to Baghdad (Jordan's principal trading partner) and Riyadh as a traditional monarchy a likely kindred spirit with common interests. King Hussein was always careful to avoid the policies of no return. As Garfinkle has observed, Jordan has adopted "management techniques that leave open the possibility of tactical reversal" (Nevo and Pappé, 1994, p. 287). Thus King Hussein's reputation for statecraft was established as he outlived and outlasted all the leaders and most of the regimes which were in power when he came to the throne. Those who attended his funeral in February 1999 were, compared to him, Johnny-come-latelys.

The mark of Hussein's achievement was that up to his death success has bred success as far as international support for Jordan is concerned. Perceived as an avowedly pro-Western, anti-communist 'Anglo-Arab' monarch the survival of King Hussein's Jordan was an important Western (or rather US/British) interest since his accession. The longer he and his regime lasted and the more he grew in stature as a significant force for moderation in the region, the more important it became to ensure his survival. He has been seen as an ally in the context of the Cold War and also as a player in the search for a settlement to the Arab-Israeli dispute. In the early days it was Britain whose subsidy was an essential contribution to Jordanian finances. British military equipment predominated in the armed forces, up to the dismissal by King Hussein of the commander General Glubb ('Glubb Pasha') and other senior British officers in 1956. This in itself was an early example of the young King exploiting popular sentiment to strengthen his credentials as an Arab nationalist. Following the Suez débâcle and the abrogation of the 1948 Anglo-Jordanian Treaty in 1957 the Americans stepped into the breach. Mostly in furtherance of the March 1957 'Eisenhower Doctrine' – promising support to anti-communist regimes – Washington took over the responsibility of helping to subsidise Jordan and also became a major arms supplier and military trainer. Moreover, the United States became, in Garfinkle's words "Jordan's protector of last resort" (Nevo and Pappé, 1994, p. 286). Although it was British rather than American troops which were rushed out to Jordan when its stability appeared at risk following the overthrow of King Feisal's Hashemite regime in Baghdad in July 1958, this was as a junior partner in an Anglo-American joint operation. (The Americans simultaneously sent forces to the Lebanon.) Keeping faith with their Hashemite protégées, Washington marked the accession of King Abdullah II with further pledges of substantial financial assistance.

Later, Arab states, notably Saudi Arabia, provided subsidies to Jordan as a 'front-line state' in the confrontation with Israel. It was these Arab subsidies, together with cheap oil from the Gulf, and remittances from expatriate Jordanian/Palestinians, which were amongst the casualties of Jordan's policy of non-involvement in Operation Desert Storm in 1990–91. This loss of revenue would have been disastrous in the past, but as explained in the chapter on the economy, thanks to the favourable verdict on King Hussein's, high profile policies by the developed world – especially as a peace-maker since the treaty with Israel in 1994 – Jordan attracted a disproportionate (for a country of its size) amount of international financing. The International Financial Institutions (IFIs), the United States, the European Union and the Japanese, have more than plugged the gap created by the desertion of traditional Arab benefactors. They have done so both in the context of an economic restructuring programme in the traditional IMF/IBRD mould and for the sake underpinning the Middle East Peace Process (MEPP) and in recognition of Jordan's contribution to it.

Having been under considerable pressure domestically in the 1950s and 1960s King Hussein did not have to face a serious sustained challenge to his authority until the expulsion of the Palestinian leadership in 1971. There have been other crises but not regime-threatening ones. As in foreign affairs, the late King was the main if not the sole policy maker. He ruled as well as reigned. He grew in confidence after he weathered the storms of 1970–71. Since then internal threats have been effectively repressed, allowing the regime to adopt a more visibly relaxed attitude to law and order and a measure of constitutional liberalisation. Occasionally 'plots' were discovered and exploited to maintain popular support for the government with outside forces blamed for encouraging internal dissent. Apart from the odd blip the country's human rights record has compared favourably with most other Arab countries. Jordan does not have the atmosphere of a police state yet such perceptions remain relative in a region often characterised in the West by a reputation for authoritarian and undemocratic rule. Since 1989 there have been impressive advances in political liberalisation: universal adult suffrage, state licensing of political parties and a national assembly with, in theory, increased powers of legislation. Press freedom also compares favourably with the limits imposed by most other Arab governments, but it is far from absolute and is corralled at times of perceived crisis. Such 'crises', however, have meant a limit on any meaningful debate about succession, the issue of Jordanian-Iraqi relations, criticism about the levels of corruption within the Hashemite regime, debate about the alleged power and importance of Islamist personalities and coalitions within the country.

Over all this King Hussein used to preside. Up to his death at 63 he remained very much in charge. His son has inherited his father's position at the centre of the system but cannot yet expect to enjoy either his prestige or his effortless authority. Both attributes will have to be earned. Moreover, under Abdullah II the Royal Court which services the King and his closest advisers may no longer remain the sole seat of power. Some of the centre of gravity will initially shift to the Prime Minister's office and to individual ministries. The King will continue to appoint Prime Ministers and we suspect that as under Hussein, ministers and civil servants will be shuffled, sometimes with the same bewildering rapidity that marked the *ancien regime*. Old habits are the hardest to break and it is probable that once Abdullah II feels in control, the centre of gravity of decision making, even on fairly trivial matters, will remain very high.

Time will tell if Jordan under King Abdullah II will become less of a paper democracy. It has been well called a 'monarchical democracy' (i.e. constitutionally a democratic structure but closely shepherded by the King) as this reflected the then King's own views on the future shape of his country. In guiding it he remained visibly anxious for it to work. On occasion he all too obviously became impatient and irritated when factors such as growing domestic opposition to normalisation with Israel as the MEPP floundered obliged him to act undemocratically. By censoring the press for example, or interfering with the activities of professional organisations, the King was able to assert his individual vision for peace and its accompanying agenda over the entire country. Ultimately this produced mixed results *vis-à-vis* the peace process with obvious diplomatic benefits to Jordan as a state at an international level but with the majority of Jordanians sceptical and marginalised from this event at a domestic level. At the same time the late King was conscious of the need to erect a framework of government which would outlive him and ensure the survival of the Hashemite regime under a less experienced and less respected monarch. It is still too early to say if he has succeeded in the long term. For the immediate future the prospects seem reasonable.

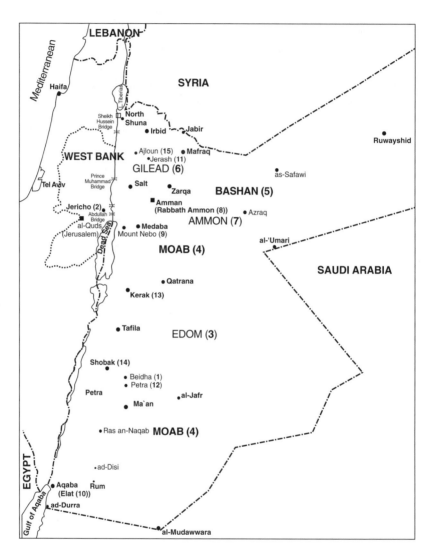

Map of Jordan

This book focuses on the Hashemite Kingdom of Jordan as part of a series on the main countries within the Middle East and North Africa (MENA) region. It is intended for a general reader, who is not necessarily a specialist, but one who has some familiarity with the main issues facing the area. The publication is intended to be a brief but comprehensive guide to Jordan and one which will suggest further reading for a more in depth study of the Hashemite Kingdom.

This volume on Jordan employs a common format to its companions in the Contemporary Middle East Series. Following the introduction the book will examine the country under five headings: (A) State formation covering the historical background to the creation of modern Jordan in 1922 and its subsequent history up to the assassination of King Abdullah in 1952. (B) Contemporary politics including the development of political life under the reign of King Hussein and contemporary pressures for democratisation. (C) The economy and its effect on the Kingdom's policies. (D) International relations and finally (E) – Whither Jordan? – An assessment of the current political and economic climate of the country and its position within the region in the new millennium.

Jordan lies in the heartland of the Arab world. It is both geographically and demographically small, making it a weak country with limited natural resources. Yet as a front line party to the Arab-Israeli conflict and as what has often been described as a pivotal state its perceived importance as a regional player is out of all proportion to its intrinsic size and power. Jordan does, in a phrase ascribed to a former British foreign minister, 'box above her weight'.

Much of the Kingdom's importance is also due to geography. Recent history and a number of demographic factors have complicated its fortuitous location, the most important being that it has the longest border with the State of Israel of any Arab country. For nearly 19 years what is now known as the 'West Bank', including east, or 'Arab' Jerusalem, was part of the Kingdom, formally annexed in 1952 as a result of the first (1948) Arab-Israeli war and lost, after less than a week's fighting in the second in June 1967. Proximity to Israel, and Jordan's rule over the West Bank from 1948 to 1967, made it the natural and unavoidable destination for hundreds thousands of Palestinian refugees in two great exoduses. The first, amounting to a large proportion of the 800,000 who fled their homes in 1948 as large areas of what became Israel were ethnically cleansed during and immediately after the war, and the second in 1967 when many of the original refugees as well as longer term inhabitants of Jordanian-ruled Palestine were once again displaced and sought refuge across the Jordan river. This wave perhaps amounted to as many as 250,000 in June-July 1967 (one quarter of the Palestinians formerly under Jordanian rule on the West Bank), swelling the ranks of the 300,000 dispossessed Palestinians already in Trans-Jordan. It was principally from that moment as Nevo and Pappé put it, that 'unlike any other state in the region, in Jordan the Arab-Israeli conflict is both a domestic and a foreign policy issue at the same time' (Nevo & Pappé, 1994, p. 1). In 1967 Jordan lost most of its control and political power over Palestinian land absorbed in 1948 but nevertheless gained a large Palestinian community in refuge east of the river, the great majority of whom, naturally enough, were more concerned with regaining their birthright than with making a contribution to their country of exile.

The instinctive ambivalence of Trans-Jordanians towards their Palestinian guests and in reverse, Palestinian ambivalence towards their hosts and their temporarily adopted King is the great fault line in Jordanian society, a line, however, increasingly blurred by the fact that (as explained in Chapter 1) a significant number of families of Palestinian origin have been in Jordan as long as and in some cases longer than some of their 'true' Trans-Jordanian neighbours. A more widespread cause of national imprecision is inter-marriage. There can be very few Jordanian families, especially in the main urban centres, that do not have Palestinian in-laws. Only one third of the 1.36 million Palestinian refugees registered with the United Nations Relief and Works Agency (UNRWA) living in Jordan (41 per cent of the total refugee population) are still in 'camps' (small houses in townships). The rest are integrated, at a variety of economic and social levels, into Jordanian society, admittedly some in places in identifiable urban areas – virtual ghettos – but with others living cheek and jowl with Jordanian neighbours. Palestinians, especially Christian Palestinians, control large parts of the private sector and are prominent throughout the professions. Only the highest ranks in the security and defence establishment are beyond Palestinian reach. In addition they remain numerically under-represented in the higher echelons of government, but have provided Prime Ministers and continue to be represented at ministerial rank (although this is generally by scions of the so-called notable families than from the ranks of the 1948 and 1967 refugees).

Since the Palestinian-Jordanian civil conflict between 1970–71 following the forcible expulsion from Jordan of the Palestinian political leadership and its more radical adherents, the Palestinian community has been generally quiescent and outwardly loyal to its adopted country. A significant proportion of them however continue to regard this adoption as a temporary status, especially many of the 400,000 or so still living in camps on the East Bank. This is despite the fact that hope of either returning to their original homes or making a new start in a viable Palestinian state become increasingly faint as time goes on. Their loyalty has been tested, especially at times when radical Arabs perceive Jordanian policies as too conciliatory towards Israel or as serving a western (perceived to be United States) agenda rather than an Arab one.

But even following the Jordanian-Israeli Peace Treaty of 1994 and as the Middle East Peace Process (MEPP) became increasingly bogged down, the Palestinians did not take to the streets. To the surprise of some observers they exhibited a much less overt rejectionist stance towards warmer Jordanian ties than many of their home grown Trans-Jordanian neighbours. In this the Palestinians living in Jordan were mainly reflecting a grudging acceptance of a policy of positive engagement with Israel, symbolised by the PLO-Israel Oslo accords of September 1993. Nevertheless, however quiescent the Palestinian community may appear and however integrated into Jordanian society it seems to be, the Jordanian government has constantly to be sensitive to possible reactions to its regional policies by a majority of the population within its borders, hence the regime's traditional and seemingly contradictory policies. On one hand, there are manifestations of pro-Western tendencies as expected of a conservative Arab monarchy and on the other, the periodic striking of radical attitudes more in keeping with its geographical position as a front line state in permanent confrontation with the 'Zionist enemy'. Accordingly the Oslo Accords and the peace treaty with Israel has narrowed Jordan's room for manoeuvre and the total collapse of the MEPP would put considerable pressure on Jordan to re-examine its relationship with Israel. We look at this possibility, amongst others, in the concluding chapter.

There are other factors which contribute to the inflated importance of Jordan as a regional player. Most significantly in recent years has been the personality and longevity of King Hussein who was on the throne from 1952 until early 1999. Throughout the bulk of that period many observers regarded King Hussein as Jordan. In common with other countries in the region – for example 'Assad's Syria' or 'Saddam's Iraq' – the image of the country is subsumed into the personality of the current ruler. Perhaps until his death this applied more so in the case of Jordan as the King had been around for so long. He was a well-known international personality. In the western media – particularly in the United States and Britain – he was often portrayed as a heroic figure: 'The Plucky Little King' as one British tabloid described him early in his reign. Courageous and enduring were the qualities commonly ascribed to him in the West. He was certainly a survivor, as is the Hashemite regime he headed. As Peter Mansfield wrote: ' Many obituaries of the Hashemite Kingdom of Jordan have been prepared for instant use. There have been many occasions in the past forty years when the external and internal forces gathered against this last of the Anglo-Arab monarchies were so strong and numerous that its survival seemed impossible. But it still lives and the obituaries gather on its files'(Mansfield, 1990, p. 417).

The obituaries have now of course appeared. Their effusive sentiments give the lie to those close observers of the Arab world in the late 1950s and throughout the 1960s, including Western ambassadors serving in Amman who were amongst those frequently predicting the imminent demise of the Hashemite monarchy. Jordan on occasions seemed doomed to share the fate of other former Arab kingdoms outside the Arabian peninsular – Egypt in 1952, Tunisia in 1957, Iraq in 1958 (the Baghdad Hashemite branch) and Libya in 1969. But as this book describes the King, over the years, legitimised and entrenched his authority and his position within the Kingdom and became virtually unassailable. The smooth succession of his hastily nominated last minute heir – Abdullah II – is an eloquent testimony to the late King's achievement in securing the position of the monarchy but presumably (with the removal of his brother Hassan who served as crown prince for over 30 years) only under whom he perceived to be the right monarch. It will be interesting to see what other 'personality regimes' in the region apart from Hashemite Jordan will survive the demise of their current reigning head of state. ('Republican' presidents Assad and Saddam have also striven to create family dynasties to seek the survival of the Alawite and Takriti succession). In complete contrast to thirty years ago Jordan, even now under a new inexperienced King, is regarded as an oasis of stability in a troubled region. This we should see as something of a (preliminary) vote of confidence in the institution as well as the incumbent.

King Hussein was partly a product of Western education –– his experiences at Harrow School in England and as an officer cadet at Sandhurst Military Academy left their mark. His English was perfect; he and his brother, the heir apparent for so long, Hassan, had an extensive network of senior and influential contacts in the West. In the King's case this had been built up over nearly 50 years. Younger Hashemites, including the present King Abdullah II, many of whom have also been educated in Europe and the United States, were encouraged to do likewise. Over time King Hussein became a credible 'Royal' in more a Western than an oriental mode, in contrast to other Arab traditional rulers of Saudi Arabia or the Gulf States. Perhaps because of the circumstances of Jordan's creation, plus the influence of his beloved grandfather King Abdullah and his own feelings with regard to where his country's best interests lie, he instinctively tended to align himself with the West in the game of nations. But as this book describes he was not always been able to do this. He was careful when his survival was at stake to bend to the pressures of Pan-Arabism or Arab nationalism, even when he believed that his or Jordan's interests might suffer. Jordan's disastrous involvement in the 1967 war is a case in point. But he could hardly have kept out of it, so strong was popular enthusiasm throughout the Arab world whipped up by President Nasser of Egypt to join forces with the Egyptians and Syrians to settle with Israel once and for all. As a result he lost half his kingdom. For similar, if more narrowly-based reasons, in 1990–91 he refused to be drawn into the Desert Storm coalition against Saddam Hussein, thus jeopardising his traditional relationship with the West and with his conservative Arab colleagues on whose financial support he relied. But on the whole his balancing act was sure footed, ensuring his position in the region, his own survival (until cancer took him, rather than a bullet) and that of his regime. King Abdullah II's skills remain largely untested, but at least the omens are more propitious than they were when his father came to the throne.

Jordan, even when boxing above its weight, has never been an Arab power of the first rank. Nor has it harboured pretensions to be one. After its annexation of the West Bank it has had no further territorial ambitions. King Abdullah I's dreams of a Hashemite dominated Greater Syria died with him. The short-lived constitutional unity between the Hashemite Kingdoms of Iraq and Jordan was one of a number of unsuccessful similar ventures – Egypt and Syria, Libya and Egypt – inspired by the concept of Pan-Arabism and not in Jordan's case for the sake of territorial aggrandisement. As the chapter on Jordan's international relationships describes, King Hussein skilfully not only manoeuvred between East and West (ensuring his true sympathies were understood where they really mattered) but also chartered a careful course between regional antagonists. He always sought to avoid isolation by attaching himself to one of the centres of power within the shifting sands of Arab power politics, now with Cairo, then with Damascus, usually with an eye cocked to Baghdad (Jordan's principal trading partner) and Riyadh as a traditional monarchy a likely kindred spirit with common interests. King Hussein was always careful to avoid the policies of no return. As Garfinkle has observed Jordan has adopted 'management techniques that leave open the possibility of tactical reversal'(Nevo and Pappé, 1994, p. 287). Thus King Hussein's reputation for statecraft was established as he outlived and outlasted all the leaders and most of the regimes which were in power when he came to the throne. Those who attended his funeral in February 1999 were, compared to him, Johnny-come-latelys.

The mark of Hussein's achievement was that up to his death success has bred success as far as international support for Jordan is concerned. Perceived as an avowedly pro-Western, anti-communist 'Anglo-Arab' monarch the survival of King Hussein's Jordan was an important Western (or rather US/British) interest since his accession. The longer he and his regime lasted and the more he grew in stature as a significant force for moderation in the region, the more important it became to ensure his survival. He has been seen as an ally in the context of the Cold War and also as a player in the search for a settlement to the Arab-Israeli dispute. In the early days it was Britain whose subsidy was an essential contribution to Jordanian finances. British military equipment predominated in the armed forces, up to the dismissal by King Hussein of the commander General Glubb ('Glubb Pasha') and other senior British officers in 1956. This in itself was an early example of the young King exploiting popular sentiment to strengthen his credentials as an Arab nationalist. Following the Suez debacle and the abrogation of the 1948 Anglo-Jordanian Treaty in 1957 the Americans stepped into the breach. Mostly in furtherance of the March 1957 'Eisenhower Doctrine' – promising support to anti-communist regimes – Washington took over the responsibility of helping to subsidise Jordan and also became a major arms supplier and military trainer. Moreover, the United States became, in Garfinkle's words 'Jordan's protector of last resort' (Nevo and Pappé, 1994, p. 286). Although it was British rather than American troops which were rushed out to Jordan when its stability appeared at risk following the overthrow of King Feisal's Hashemite regime in Baghdad in July 1958, this was as a junior partner in an Anglo-American joint operation. (The Americans simultaneously sent forces to the Lebanon). Keeping faith with their Hashemite protégées, Washington marked the accession of King Abdullah II with further pledges of substantial financial assistance.

Later, Arab states, notably Saudi Arabia, provided subsidies to Jordan as a 'front-line state' in the confrontation with Israel. It was these Arab subsidies, together with cheap oil from the Gulf, and remittances from expatriate Jordanian-Palestinians, which were amongst the casualties of Jordan's policy of non-involvement in Operation Desert Storm in 1990–91. This loss of revenue would have been disastrous in the past, but as explained in the chapter on the economy, thanks to the favourable verdict on King Hussein, high profile policies by the developed world – especially as a peace-maker since the treaty with Israel in 1994 – Jordan attracted a disproportionate (for a country of its size) amount of international financing. The International Financial Institutions (IFIs), the United States, the European Union and the Japanese, have more than plugged the gap created by the desertion of traditional Arab benefactors. They have done so both in the context of an economic restructuring programme in the traditional IMF/IBRD mould and for the sake underpinning the Middle East Peace Process (MEPP) and in recognition of Jordan's contribution to it.

Having been under considerable pressure domestically in the 1950s and 1960s King Hussein did not have to face a serious sustained challenge to his authority until the expulsion of the Palestinian leadership in 1971. There have been crises but not regime-threatening ones. As in foreign affairs, the late King was the main if not the sole policy maker. He ruled as well as reigned. He grew in confidence after he weathered the storms of 1970–71. Since then internal threats have been effectively repressed, allowing the regime to adopt a more visibly relaxed attitude to law and order and a measure of constitutional liberalisation. Occasionally 'plots' were discovered and exploited to maintain popular support for the government with outside forces blamed for encouraging internal dissent. Apart from the odd blip the country's human rights record has compared favourably with most other Arab countries. Jordan does not have the atmosphere of a police state yet such perceptions remain relative in a region often characterised in the West by a reputation for authoritarian and undemocratic rule. Since 1989 there have been impressive advances in political liberalisation, universal adult suffrage, state licensing of political parties and a national assembly with, in theory, increased powers of legislation. Press freedom also compares favourably with the limits imposed by most other Arab governments, but it is far from absolute and is corralled at times of perceived crisis. Such 'crises', however, have meant a limit on any meaningful debate about succession, the issue of Jordanian-Iraqi relations, criticism about the levels of corruption within the Hashemite regime, debate about the alleged power and importance of Islamist personalities and coalitions within the country.

Over all this King Hussein used to preside. Up to his death at 63 he remained very much in charge. His son has inherited his father's position at the centre of the system but cannot yet expect to enjoy either his prestige or his effortless authority. Both attributes will have to be earned. Moreover, under Abdullah II the Royal Court which services the King and his closest advisers may no longer remain the sole seat of power. Some of the centre of gravity will initially shift to the Prime Minister's office and to individual ministries. The King will continue to appoint Prime Ministers and we suspect that as under Hussein, ministers and civil servants will be shuffled, sometimes with the same bewildering rapidity that marked the *ancien regime*. Old habits are the hardest to break and it is probable that once Abdullah II feels in control, the centre of gravity of decision making, even on fairly trivial matters, will remain very high.

Time will tell if Jordan under King Abdullah II will become less of a paper democracy. It has been well called a 'monarchical democracy' (i.e. constitutionally a democratic structure but closely shepherded by the King) as this reflected the then King's own views on the future shape of his country. In guiding it he remained visibly anxious for it to work. On occasion he all too obviously became impatient and irritated when factors such as growing domestic opposition to normalisation with Israel as the MEPP floundered obliged him to act undemocratically. By censoring the press for example, or interfering with the activities of professional organisations, the King was able to assert his individual vision for peace and its accompanying agenda over the entire country. Ultimately this produced mixed results vis-à-vis the peace process with obvious diplomatic benefits to Jordan as a state at an international level but with the majority of Jordanians sceptical and marginalised from this event at a domestic level. At the same time the late King was conscious of the need to erect a framework of government which would outlive him and ensure the survival of the Hashemite regime under a less experienced and less respected monarch. It is still too early to say if he has succeeded in the long term. For the immediate future the prospects seem reasonable.

# Chapter 1

## THE FORMATION OF THE HASHEMITE KINGDOM
(Bracketed numbers against old-kingdom names refer to the map)

TRADITION AND ANTIQUITY

Jordan as a modern nation state has existed for less than eighty years. It occupies part of an ancient land inhabited since earliest human times; the Jordan Valley was once the home of Palaeolithic and Mesolithic hunter-gatherers. A Neolithic people introduced agriculture and a settled way of life into the region seven to eight thousand years Before Christ. Beidha (1) on the East Bank of the Jordan and Jericho (2) on the West are on the sites of settlements which date back to some of this region's earliest cities.

Over the subsequent millenniums fresh invasions followed. Most significantly in 2000 BC the Amorites, Semitic nomads from central Arabia, destroyed the urban culture and having adopted the settled life gradually assimilated the people they conquered into what became known as Canaan. During the fifteenth to thirteenth centuries BC tribal kingdoms familiar to readers of the Old Testament emerged in the region as a result of the conflict between two great powers: the Hittite, from what is now Turkey, and the Egyptians. Of these the towns and settlements of Edom (3), Moab (4), Bashan (5), Gilead (6) and Ammon (7) made up much of what is now contemporary Jordan. Ammon-or at least its capital Rabbath Ammon (8) has lent its name to the modern capital city of Hashemite Jordan–Amman.

Other incursions and conquests followed. The Israelite exodus, led by Moses, passed East of the Jordan before crossing the river further north. Moses was reputedly buried on Mount Nebo (9) (20 miles south of Amman) after his tantalising glimpse of the Promised Land. Ironically, given the events of the twentieth century, the Israelites subsequently met stiff resistance from the Philistines, an Eastern Mediterranean people who gave their name to Palestine (ancient Philistia) or *falistin* in Arabic. Subsequently part of the lands east of the Jordan came under the control of Israelite Kings. Solomon (961–922 BC) exploited the mineral wealth of Edom (3) and built a port (Elat (10)) to import spice from the East on a site possibly coinciding with modern Aqaba.

After Solomon the Jewish Kingdom split into two: Israel and Judah (Judea) with it capital at Jerusalem. Centuries of invasion and conflict followed. First the Assyrians under whom much of what is now Jordan was divided into provinces – serving as buffer areas to contain the desert tribes, a practice followed by a succession of foreign rulers. These included the neo-Babylonian empire in Mesopotamia. Nebuchadnezzar destroyed Jerusalem in 586 BC and transported the Jewish population to Babylon. They were returned under the Persian Cyrus II and the region became part of the Achaemenid empire until the advent of Alexander the Great in 334 BC. Following his death his Macedonian generals split his empire between them (founding the Ptolemite pharaohs in Egypt and the Seleucid rulers in Syria) with the Jordan region coming under the control of the Ptolemies; Amman – the city of seven hills – was renamed Philadelphia in honour of the Pharaoh Ptolemy Philadelphus. Greek settlers with their Hellenistic culture left their stamp on urban centres and traces can still be seen in such places as Jerash (11) (Garasa) and Amman.

The Syrian based Seleucids who displaced their rivals the Ptolemies in 198 BC were themselves the victims of Nabataean (Arabs who had settled in Edom in the 7th Century BC) expansion. The spectacular remains of Petra (12) – biblical Sela – commemorate their achievements, which included the control of a desert empire stretching from Syria to the Red Sea. They retreated in the face of growing Roman power and in 106 AD Trajan incorporated Petra into the Roman Empire but allowed the Nabataeans to continue to flourish under Roman rule. Following the partition of the Roman Empire in 395 AD the Jordan region formed part of the Byzantine Empire ruled from Constantinople.

Christianity was widely practised in the towns and continued to be under the Christian Arabs. For example, the warrior nomad Ghassanids, loyal to Constantinople and who controlled the region from the sixth century and acted as a buffer against waves of other Arabs moving up from the south – a dam that failed to hold back the advancing tide of Islamic expansion from 636 AD onwards.

ISLAM AND ARAB RULE TO THE OTTOMANS

By the time the Prophet Mohammed died in 632 AD he, his immediate successors – The Four Rightly Guided Caliphs – and followers had stamped their authority on most of the tribes of the Arabian Peninsular. The new monotheistic religion of Islam envisaged uniting the individual believer, the state and society under the omnipotent will of God. Thus Islamic rulers were permitted to exercise both temporal and spiritual authority. Followers of Islam, called Muslims, collectively formed *Dar al-Islam* (the house of Islam). Four years after Mohammed's death, as the result of the decisive battle on the banks of the Yarmuk river – today part of the Jordanian/Syrian border – all Syria fell to the Muslim Arabs. What is now Jordan was administered in two units known as Junds – the north and west from Tiberias (*Jund al-Urdun*) and the rest from Damascus (*Jund Dimashq*).

Despite the original zeal for conversion, the Islamic conquests did not result in the eradication of Christianity among the Arabs of the Syrian region – which included present day Jordan. Indeed, according to some historians, they might not have been a numerical minority until the end of the Crusades. (Salibi, 1993, p. 18). But over the years their numbers steadily declined as the result of the growth of the Muslim population swollen by fresh Arab and non-Arab Muslim immigration. There was also increasing Christian emigration, but by the beginning of the 20th Century Christians in the Trans-Jordanian highlands still formed about 15 per cent of the population. Today the figure is under 5 per cent with continuing emigration mostly to North America and Australia.

Two successive Muslim dynasties followed, ruled by 'Rightly Guided Caliphs' claiming linear descent from the Prophet (recognised as such by the Sunnis but not by the Shi'a, following a schism over an earlier disputed succession to the caliphate which has persisted to today). They controlled the region from Damascus. The Ummayyads (whose magnificent mosque in Damascus is their most striking memorial) were followed in 750 AD by the Abbasids who moved the capital of the caliphate to Baghdad. They subsequently lost the Jordan area to Shi'ite Fatimid caliphs in Egypt, who were in their turn displaced by Seljuk Turks in 1071 having also ousted the Abbasids from Baghdad. It was their perceived threat to the Christian Byzantine Empire as well as a desire to seize the holy places in Palestine from the Muslims, which sparked off Pope Urban II's call for the launch of the Crusades.

According to some historians, throughout much of this time the Jordan area remained a backwater. (Rinehart, 1980, p. 11) Traditional camel routes lost out to seaborne trade with the exception of the main Muslim pilgrim route to Mecca from Damascus. The modern desert highway from Amman to Aqaba follows in the steps of those early pilgrims. Much of the bedouinization of Jordan dates from this period, as towns became depopulated and sedentary agricultural communities decayed. The Crusades left their mark on what the crusaders called

*Outre Jourdain* (beyond Jordan – possibly the origin of the description Transjordan), as did the Arab armies opposing them. The castles of Karak (13) and Shobak (14) in southern Jordan are Crusader foundations, whilst that of Ajlun (15) in the north is an Arab creation attributed to Saladin. His decisive victory over the crusaders (or Franks as they were known locally) in 1187 at Hattin (near Lake Tiberias) meant the beginning of the end of the Latin Kingdom of Jerusalem, despite the temporary re-occupation of the coastal strip between Jaffa and Beirut during the Third Crusade.

Following Saladin's death his successors quarrelled amongst themselves and the Ayyubid dynasty was split up into a number of petty principalities until the dynasty was overthrown by the Mamluks (a caste of slave-soldiers, many of Kurdish and Circassian origin). Under the expansionist rule of warrior sultans, by the late 14th century they held sway between the Nile to the Euphrates. But in their turn, weakened by internal divisions, they succumbed to the dynamic and aggressive Ottoman Empire when in 1517 Mamluk Egypt and its possessions, including the Jordan region, were annexed by the Ottoman Sultan Selim I.

## OTTOMAN RULE TO THE BRITISH MANDATE

The Jordan region continued to stagnate under Ottoman rule (Rinehart, 1980, p. 14). Pilgrim caravans to Mecca brought in some revenue to those who lived near its route, but otherwise the East Bank was largely ignored by the outside world until 19th century European travellers 'rediscovered' such places as Petra. The Ottoman Turks administered their territories through governors in charge of *vilayets* (provinces) but control in the East Bank, regarded as marginal to imperial interests, was lax and military garrisons small. The one significant development was the construction of the Hijaz railway by the Turks, with German assistance. Started in 1900, by 1908 it linked Damascus with the holy city of Medina, traversing the territory between the two in what would become modern-day Jordan. This facilitated the pilgrim traffic and Turkish military control of the Arabian peninsular. Turkish military garrisons protected the railway and tribal sheikhs were paid stipends for the same purpose.

Throughout the latter Ottoman period the Bedouin tribes including, for example, the Bani Hassan, the Adwan, the Huwaytat and the Bani Sakhr (whose successors still live in modern Jordan) frequently revolted against the authorities – most notably in 1905 and 1910, and were only suppressed with great difficulty. In the late 19th century the Ottomans had encouraged the settlement of Circassian farmers around Amman in an attempt to pacify the region. Circassian emigration continued into the area until 1909 as Russian persecution of these Sunni Moslems continued in the Caucasus. Their descendants continue to fill senior appointments in modern Jordan – especially in the armed forces.

The last two decades of the 19th century saw the emergence of two political movements destined to be on a collision course. Arab nationalism – as part of a movement known as the Arab revival – and Zionism. Both movements aimed at uniting their people in a national homeland. They were to converge and confront each other in Palestine and despite the hopes of those (relatively few idealists) that believed that both traditions could grow up together in an atmosphere of mutual accommodation, they were to prove incompatible. The Arab revival started primarily as an intellectual cultural movement, initially based in Beirut, encouraging the study of Arab history, culture and language in pursuit of an 'Arab identity'. This quickly developed into a nationalist movement opposing Ottoman-non-Arab authority, looking for autonomy or even independence for an 'Arab nation' rather than for an identifiable nation state in the modern sense.

More or less simultaneously a Jewish revival was gathering force in Europe, calling for the return of the Jews in the Diaspora to their historic homeland. The prime mover was Theodor Herzl whose book *The Jewish State* argued the case for a Jewish homeland in the absence of which he believed the Jews would always remain a people apart – rootless and unwelcome everywhere. Herzl convened the First Zionist Congress in 1897, leading to the foundation of the Zionist Organisation with the aim of creating a home in Palestine for the Jewish people 'secured by public law'. The organisation facilitated Jewish immigration from Europe into Palestine where by 1914 the number of Jews had risen significantly to 85,000 – about 12 per cent of the total population. The community had evolved a distinctive system of communal living, primarily agricultural, but including the building of the new city of Tel Aviv founded in 1909.

Meanwhile, as Europe moved towards war the old Ottoman system was swept away by reforming nationalist officers known as the Young Turks. Their programme of increased and more effective centralised rule of Ottoman territory and aggressive 'Turkification' intensified Arab opposition, particularly amongst the educated and politically ambitious city dwellers who felt they were being turned from Ottoman citizens into

Turkish subjects. Less politically articulate perhaps but more traditional resentment grew amongst the desert tribes of the Arabian peninsular – including the Jordan region – fearing that stronger government would interfere with their cherished way of life.

The link between the urban nationalists and the desert tribesmen was Sharif Hussein bin Ali, the Emir of Mecca, hereditary custodian of the Muslim holy places of Mecca and Medina. As head of the Hashemite branch of the Quraysh tribe, Hussein claimed descent from the Prophet. Hussein's sons, however, were eager to embrace the message of nationalism promoted in the elite circles they frequented. Sharif Hussein's son Abdullah probably made his first contacts with Arab nationalist underground groups operating in Beirut and Damascus during the fifteen-year period he spent studying and growing up in Istanbul. His younger brother Feisal – a fellow national-ist – had delivered the 'Damascus Protocol' to his father, appealing to Hussein as 'Father of the Arabs' to secure them independence from the Turks and setting out the nationalist's demands –subsequently used by Feisal in his negotiations with the British. In exchange the national-ists accepted the Hashemites as spokesmen for the Arab cause. Nationalism would open a path by which the Hashemites could underpin their Islamic credentials in a modern era of rising national secularism and the movement for Arab independence.

According to Mary Wilson, Sherif Hussein's ambitions from 1908 until the outbreak of war were 'quite simple and constant'. 'An autonomous, hereditary emirate in the Hijaz, one that would be safe against Ottoman administrative encroachments on the one hand but that would enjoy Ottoman favour over neighbouring principalities on the other' (Wilson, 1987, p. 25). His son Abdullah had been the main go-between with the Ottomans between 1908 and 1914 and it was Abdullah who made the first contacts with the British just before and immediately after the start of hostilities in Europe in August 1914. With the Ottoman Empire siding with the Central Powers (Germany and Austria), the British were anxious to pre-empt any attempt by the Turks to persuade the Arabs to proclaim a *Jihad* (Islamic Holy war) in support of the Ottoman Empire and its allies. Sherif Hussein, as Emir of Mecca, was the key figure in this. The British, via Abdullah, knew of Hussein's ambitions both for himself and as the champion of Arab nationalism. A mutuality of interest was not difficult to establish. And although Hussein maintained contact with Istanbul he decided that the British had more to offer than the Turks to further his ambitions, which had by now gone beyond mere autonomy within an Ottoman imperial framework.

Three sets of documentation drafted between July 1915 and November 1917 were to determine the political geography and history of the Middle East in the immediate post-war years. The first, known as the Hussein-McMahon correspondence, was an exchange of eight letters between Sherif Hussein and Sir Henry McMahon, the British High Commissioner in Egypt, from July 1915 and January 1916. This exchange was intended to establish spheres of territorial interest between Hussein and Britain and her allies. The British undertakings were in many cases vague, especially regarding those areas not to be under Arab control. These included places 'not purely Arab', such as Baghdad and Basra where the British had a particular claim or territory where France might have special interests. Areas of disagreement were left for settlement later, but Hussein was satisfied that he had British support for post-war Arab independence and proclaimed the Arab revolt (and himself as King of the Arabs) in June 1916. But sadly for Arab ambitions, a month before the French and British governments had concluded the secret Sykes-Picot agreement which although allowing for a post-war Arab state in Arabia, divided most of the rest of the Ottoman possessions in the Levant/Fertile Crescent between them. (Imperial Russia, which subsequently ratified the agreement, also benefited in gaining territory in the north-east of the Empire. However, their successors the Bolshevik revolutionaries disowned and denounced the arrangements). Jerusalem was to be under ill-defined international control and parts of Palestine were excluded.

The third document was the Balfour Declaration of November 1917. This was a letter written on 2 November 1917 by Lord Arthur Balfour, the British Foreign Secretary, to Lord Rothschild the leader of British Jewry. Balfour made it known that ' His Majesty's Government views with favour the establishment in Palestine of a national home for the Jewish people as long as it did not prejudice the civil and religious rights of existing non-Jewish communities [there.]' Recognising the growing influence of the Zionist movement within the Jewish communities in Europe and North America, British strategists thought that the promise of a 'national home' would prove to turn the Jews into a trump card. Particularly so in the United States where they could bring their weight to bear in favour of entering the war against Germany and her central European allies. To Zionists such as Chaim Weizmann, the organisation's principal leader, the Declaration, despite its reference to safeguarding the rights of the 'non-Jewish communities' (i.e. the vast majority), was a firm promise of British support for a future Jewish state, not a mere home. These same carefully worded reassurances notwithstanding, to generations of Arabs the Balfour Declaration has equally been seen as a betrayal of promises given to Sherif Hussein and the other leaders of the Arab Revolt. Thus the gibe: 'the twice promised land' has some validity in reference to the creation of post-war Palestine. Whatever Britain's real long term intentions in drafting the Declaration (if indeed any were thought through) its basic contradictions conspired to make its future administration of the Mandate for Palestine – of which more below – something of a mission impossible.

In November 1917, seventeen months after the Arab Revolt got under way, the new Bolshevik Government in Russia revealed the contents of the Sykes-Picot agreement. Britain hastened to reassure the Arabs that commitments made to them would be honoured. The Revolt, sponsored, substantially armed and bank rolled by the British was going well for the Allies at that time which may have helped the Arab leadership to shrug off any suspicions that they were to be shortchanged. Feisal had captured the port town of Aqaba in July 1917; General Allenby and his British forces took Jerusalem in December and then systematically occupied the rest of Palestine and what would become known as Transjordan in preparation for an advance on Damascus. The decisive British victory in September 1918 over the Turks at Megiddo (now in Israel) facilitated this move. More or less simultaneously Arab forces commanded by Colonel T.E. Lawrence ('Lawrence of Arabia' who fought throughout the Revolt with the Arabs) captured Daraa on the modern Jordan/Syria border. Feisal then entered Damascus on 2 October. The armistice of 31 October ended the campaign in the Near East. A campaign which Sherif Hussein and his sons had seen as a major war of liberation with British support would not bring all the spoils of victory which they believed had been promised them. From the British perspective the Arab army was an adjunct to the main offensive in Palestine, diverting Turkish attention and resources on the fringe of the serious fighting. Even Lawrence, who was not a man to denigrate his role and that of his Arab allies, once referred to the Arab Revolt as a 'side-show to a side-show'. But he may have been selling the Arabs short. Most military historians would agree that the activities of Feisal and his 'Northern Arab Army', protecting the British right flank and creating upheaval in the Turkish rear echelon by tying up 30,000 troops, made a major contribution to winning the war against the Turks (Abu Nowar, 1989, p. 10).

## THE CREATION OF TRANSJORDAN

Apart from the capture of Aqaba in July 1917 and the virtually unopposed occupation of Amman by the Arab armies led by Feisal in September 1918, what is now modern Jordan saw little of the Arab revolt. The area was included in the sphere of influence allocated to Britain in the Sykes-Picot treaty. Zionists were also to argue that the East Bank of the Jordan was envisaged as part of the Jewish National Home envisaged in the Balfour Declaration. At any event, at the end of the war this remote, thinly populated and mostly barren territory was not looked on as a separate unit (Lawless, 1998, p. 629). Post-war action centred initially on Damascus, where Feisal with the assistance of Iraqi nationalists and British officers had set up an autonomous government. In so doing they had been encouraged by the Anglo-French declaration of 7 November 1918 favouring the establishment of indigenous administrations in Iraq and Syria.

Sadly for Arab ambition autonomy was one thing, independence quite another as far as the victorious European allies were concerned. In July 1919 the Syrian General Congress meeting in Damascus called for an allied recognition of an independent Syria (including Palestine) with Feisal as its king. (The congress subsequently proclaimed Abdullah as King of Iraq). These pronouncements being ignored by the Allies, Feisal himself pressed his case at the Paris Peace Conference, claiming Syria on 'the strength of the Hussein-McMahon correspondence, Arab services to the Allies during the war and his existing administration' (Wilson, 1987, p. 40).

Fearing their inability to control an 'independent' Feisal (thought to be dangerously Anglophile) the French persuaded their British allies to adhere to the Sykes-Picot agreement which had placed Syria (excluding Palestine) in the French sphere of influence. At the same conference the mandate system was approved (a compromise between the direct rule of Imperialist powers disliked by the Americans and the prospect of emerging indigenous self-government). This formula allowed Britain and France to divide much of the Middle East between them at the 1920 San Reno conference in furtherance of their strategic interests in the region, Britain getting mandatory control of Palestine and Iraq, the French Syria and Lebanon. The British withdrew their troops from Syria in favour of French soldiers who enforced Feisal's withdrawal from Damascus. His consolation prize was to be installed by the British as King of Iraq less than a year later.

Having settled Feisal in Baghdad the problem facing the British was the future of his brother Abdullah. He had set off from the Hijaz where he had recently suffered a humiliating defeat at the hands of Bin Saud's *ikhwan* warriors at Turaba – a battle which was to foreshadow the eventual complete takeover of Hashemite possessions in the Hijaz by the Saudis. More immediately they had shattered his dreams of an Arabian empire (Wilson, 1987, p. 36). His new objective was to organise resistance against the French in Syria – having failed to get the British to agree to him accepting the throne of Iraq, which at that point had not yet been awarded to his brother Feisal. He arrived in Ma'an (now in southern Jordan) with a handful of tribal followers. They presented no immediate military threat to the French who were busy establishing themselves in Syria. Abdullah's presence was however an embarrassment to the British who had set up a rudimentary administration (guided by a handful of political officers resident in strategic places) in the Transjordan region, pending a decision on whether it should be placed under a separate military government or (as some officials wanted) incorporated into the Mandate for Palestine. After three months in Ma'an Abdullah moved northwards to Amman, explaining to the British authorities in Jerusalem that he had come to bring order to Transjordan which had fallen into anarchy following the enforced exile of his brother Feisal by the French in Damascus.

The British, reluctant to use force to dislodge Abdullah, decided to make a virtue out of a virtual *fait accompli*. Accordingly, at the Cairo conference in March 1921 chaired by Winston Churchill, Secretary of State for the Colonies, it was decided to confirm Feisal as King of Iraq and make Abdullah responsible for an Arab government in Transjordan for an initial period of six months at an annual subsidy of £5,000. According to Wilson, Abdullah was told that if he succeeded in curbing anti-French feeling during his six months this would bring him into French good books and strengthen his chances of being installed as Emir in Damascus (Wilson, 1987, p. 53). This condition was something that the British would work for in his support. It was a tempting prospect for a man who made no secret of his territorial ambitions, who was disappointed by the collapse of Hashemite plans for Arabia and whose suggestion that he should unite Palestine and Transjordan into an Arab Emirate had not found favour with the

British. Indeed for the rest of his life Abdullah strove for wider horizons than those provided by his poor and tiny kingdom – a driving ambition which motivated many of his policies throughout his reign. Ambitions as James Morris put it 'were constantly bubbling, for Transjordan was a very small principality for so ample a prince'. (Morris, 1959, p. 117) Ultimately his desire for a larger role, as exemplified by his dialogue with the Zionist movement and subsequently with the government of the state of Israel, was to lead to his assassination by Arab radicals (Schlaim, 1990).

The British had doubts about Abdullah's competence but in the end it was thought easier and above all cheaper to leave him where he was. The British government subsequently informally confirmed his position. In September 1922 the League of Nations formally excepted Transjordan from the provisions of the Mandate of Palestine – a decision challenged by the Zionists from the beginning and not accepted by some of their more radical adherents to this day. In May 1923 Britain formally recognised the Emirate of Transjordan as an 'independent constitutional state' under the rule of Emir Abdullah with British tutelage (Lawless, 1998, p. 630). Subsequently in 1925 when Ibn Saud forced the abdication of Sherif Hussein's son Ali, as King of the Hijaz, Abdullah took advantage of the defeat of a Saudi Wahabi raiding party by mainly Bani Sakhr tribesmen into Transjordan to incorporate Ma'an and Aqaba into his dominions (Abu Nowar, 1989, p. 77). The new Saudi rulers of the Hijaz and Nejd did not challenge this annexation (although they continued to resent it) and in consequence the southern borders of the country would, apart from one small adjustment, remain unaltered to modern times.

## THE DEVELOPMENT OF TRANSJORDAN 1921–1939

As with the other Arab states created as a result of the post war settlement, the borders of Transjordan were arbitrary and showed scant respect for grazing and other tribal traditions. Early statistics should be treated with some caution but it is likely that the new state had a population of over 300,000 once Ma'an and Aqaba had been brought within the expanded state. Excluding these areas the population in 1922 was 225,000: 54 per cent 'settled' and the rest 'nomadic'. (Not a clear-cut distinction; some nomads practised part-time agriculture and some peasants were semi-nomadic). It was, however, more ethnically homogenous than any of the other mandated states, with Arabs making up over 94 per cent of the population. The only significant non-Arab ethnic groups were the Circassians at just under 5 per cent, but they had Sunni Islam in common with their Arab Muslim neighbours. Christian Arabs formed about 10 per cent of Transjordanians – Greek Orthodox and Greek Catholic being the most numerous. Inter-communal relations were generally good – disputes would more likely be over land than religious or ethnic reasons (Wilson, 1987, p. 56). Virtually everyone was identified by family, clan and tribal affiliation, forming a social organisation which had been created by lack of urbanisation and distance from centres of power or economic influence. In short the rulers of the new state would have to expend considerable energy in creating and establishing a new level of national identity which was Jordanian in character and yet managed to respect pre-existing loyalties and ties. Indeed, over successive decades the Hashemites engaged in what Anderson refers to as the construction of an 'imagined community', a form of national identity and nationalism whose foundations lay in historical myth and a rolling definition of what it means to be Jordanian (Anderson, 1983).

The majority of people – perhaps 80 per cent – lived outside the main towns. Salt, the biggest, had 20,000 inhabitants in 1920. Amman was little more than a large village with a population of 2,400 but steadily expanded when Abdullah expressed a preference for it as his capital. The balance of the population were farmers in village communities and pastoral nomadic or semi-nomadic tribesmen. Profitable cultivation was confined to the Jordan valley and a narrow strip of land on the adjoining highlands to the East. Scarcity of water determined the pattern of cultivation. The only river water came from the Jordan and its two tributaries, the Zarqa and the Yarmuk. Rainfall ranged from 40cm in the Ajlun area, which supported lush agriculture, to less than 5cm in the eastern desert – the Badia.

It was upon this landscape and its people who had lived for generations within a strictly hierarchical tribal society that Abdullah asserted his authority. With the help of British officials holding many of the key positions in the fledgling bureaucracy and a treasury dependent on a small British subsidy he put together his administration. His first 'cabinet' – an executive council – was mostly composed of nationalists who had served his brother Feisal in Damascus. They almost had the appearance of a Syrian 'government-in-exile' symbolising, according to Wilson, Abdullah's restless ambitions 'to move on to Damascus' (Wilson, 1987, p. 62). As time went on Abdullah, under local tribal pressure, brought in Transjordanian notables whilst balancing the conflicting interests of the nationalists and British advisers. The latter strongly favoured the inclusion of locals at the expense of Syrian nationalists whose commitment to Transjordan was uncertain and who appeared to feed Abdullah's territorial expansionist ideas.

Despite the formal references to Transjordan's 'independence' it was all too apparent to Abdullah that he would continue to be dependent on British financial and military support to maintain his newly created entity. He was thus compelled to live with Britain's formal insistence that Transjordan was a district rather than an Emirate as Abdullah himself preferred to refer to his kingdom. For the period up to 1939 Britain provided about one third of total yearly revenue. The initial level of subsidy or grant-in-aid was set at £150,000 per year. In exchange for this support the British government – through the office of the High Commissioner (for Palestine) in Jerusalem – insisted on exercising a considerable degree of financial control. For example, stringent budget cuts were imposed from 1923 to 1926 with Abdullah's Civil List progressively reduced from £36,000 to £12,000.

Any newly-created state will seek stability through the maintenance of its military strength and the British were aware that it was imperative that in order to prevent Abdullah from breaking out on his own the military control of Transjordan would have to remain in their hands. To maintain security the British had authorised and helped to train a small (1,300 all ranks) military force which came formally into being in 1923 as the Arab Legion. This was a separate unit to the Transjordanian Frontier Force (TJFF), raised later and also under formal British command. Nominally the Emir was Commander in Chief of the Arab Legion but a British officer exercised the day to day command and control. The first commander was General Frederick Peake (Peake Pasha) who was succeeded in 1939 by his deputy, the better known General John Glubb (Glubb Pasha) who remained in charge until his dismissal by Abdullah's grandson King Hussein in 1956. Thus, on the military side British Royal Air Force (RAF) aircraft had to be deployed in the early 1920s not only to repel a number of further Saudi-based Wahabi attacks, but also to put down a serious tribal revolt by the Adwan. As all equipment was British and with senior ranks filled by Britons it was His Majesty's Government in London rather than Abdullah who had ultimate control of the Legion. In practice, in Abdullah's time the relationship with both Peake and Glubb worked well as a genuine partnership between the palace and the military but one under which Abdullah could clearly never usurp Britain's ultimate control.

From 1924 onwards the various administrative instruments associated with the development of a modern state and society gradually made their appearance. The erection of settled borders and the steady absorption of immigrant communities shaped the structure of Transjordan's social and political landscape. Migrants included a large influx of Syrians and Hizajis fleeing unrest in their own territories. Abdullah imported a number of Palestinians, some on secondment from the Mandate administration and placed them in positions of responsibility in the bureaucracy where they and British colleagues headed most of the technical departments of state. In the absence of trained Transjordanians, Palestinians and Syrians filled the posts of teachers, surveyors, medical and agricultural officers. Many senior members of today's Palestinian/Jordanian establishment trace their arrival on the East bank from that time, including the Al Rifa'i family who have provided the country with two Prime Ministers and many top civil servants. Communications although still primitive improved steadily with the repair and expansion of the northern portion of the Hijaz Railway. These developments were reflected in the expansion of the capital Amman which by 1925–6 had a population of 20,000.

## CONSTITUTIONAL DEVELOPMENT

The two major agreements governing the relationship between Britain and Transjordan up to the Second World War were enacted in 1923 and 1928. The first has been briefly referred to above and recognised Transjordan as a 'national state being prepared for independence' (Nyrop, 1980, p. 22). The agreement promised British recognition of Transjordanian independence provided the government was 'constitutional' and permitted the British government to 'fulfil their international obligations in respect of the territory' (Abu Nowar, 1989, p. 83). Whatever the weasel wording and the clauses enshrining British financial control, Abdullah regarded the document as endorsing Transjordan's independence and had it celebrated as such. From the British viewpoint the agreement had the desired effect of pressurising Abdullah towards constitutional reform – a process he had resisted up to then. From the beginning he had been very reluctant to surrender any of his extremely limited powers to any legislative body.

On 20 February 1928 a second agreement, in the form of the Anglo-Transjordanian Treaty, was signed in Jerusalem. Under its provisions the British retained control over many crucial activities: foreign affairs, armed forces, communications and state finances. Wilson described the treaty as 'inequality written into every clause' but a price Abdullah was happy to pay despite considerable popular opposition to it (Wilson, 1987, p. 102). A British resident representative (the Resident) was to be stationed in Amman reporting to the High Commissioner for Transjordan in Jerusalem who, in his other capacity, remained responsible for the separate mandate for Palestine (Abu Nowar, 1989, pp. 286–290). Transjordan was 'promoted' from a district to an Emirate and the British subsidy was secured (in principle, at least) indefinitely. This treaty included provision for a constitution setting up an independent government which, was subsequently promulgated as the Transjordan Organic Law.

This law was to be the basis of the 1952 Constitution (as amended by further measures of constitutional advance in 1939 and 1946) adopted during King Talal's brief reign. According to Abu Nowar it was 'nearly synonymous with the numerous written constitutions framed by Britain for her overseas colonies on their attainment of independence' (Abu Nowar, 1989, p. 206). It followed closely the constitution drawn up for the other British-backed Hashemite 'monarchy' in Iraq. And like many other examples it incorporated '[British] concepts of government by qualified and essentially limited constitutional institutions with manageable democratic freedoms' (Abu Nowar, 1989, p. 207). The preamble to the Organic Law referred to Jordan as 'the whole independent country of Trans-Jordan' (sic) and the British role was formally limited to advice any law concerning matters covered by the Anglo-Transjordanian Treaty. The constitution established a Legislative Council, a (non-elected) Executive Council and an independent judiciary covering civil, religious and special courts.

The Legislative Council had provision for 21 members – 14 elected from three urbanised constituencies (males over 18 having the vote), 2 appointed tribal representatives put forward by tribal commissions (the Bedouin were not formally enfranchised for largely practical reasons) plus the Chief Minister and four of the appointed Executive Council members. Minorities were over represented with four Christians and two Circassians – six out of fourteen elected members. The Legislative Council had some teeth being able to reject legislation as they did with the 1931 budget, but only as an act of defiance apparently encouraged by Abdullah to put pressure on the British to increase their subsidy to the country (Wilson, 1987, p. 97).

The constitution had some interesting and enlightened features including safeguards for personal rights and freedoms including those of speech, assembly, opinion and religion. Freedom from arbitrary arrest, property rights and the principle of non-interference in the courts was also enshrined in the new law. Muslim courts had exclusive jurisdiction in matters of personal status over all Muslims and the provisions of Shari'a (Islamic) Law applied in these cases. Non-Muslims were protected through an entitlement to opt for the jurisdiction of the civil courts in disputes with Muslims. A reference in the preamble to Transjordan having Islam as its official religion, which appeared in a draft produced by a constitutional committee, was omitted from the final document.

### LAND REFORM AND THE ARMED FORCES

Two other important developments marked the inter-war period. The first was substantial land reform conducted by the British-led Department of Lands and Surveys. Land ownership was determined and large blocs of common held land (mainly tribal communal ownership) was broken up into smaller plots and distributed to individuals. Land taxes were reassessed and harmonised. According to Wilson the British wanted to create a 'stable class of small and medium-sized peasant landowners' with a stake in the Emirate and discourage the formation of huge estates as had occurred in Iraq (Wilson, 1987, p. 98). Some large landowners did emerge from this process – mostly leading tribal sheikhs. This group was joined by Abdullah himself in 1931 when at the suggestion of the British he was awarded extensive estates to bolster his personal income and thus supplement a meagre civil list, which as mentioned above was constantly being trimmed by the British Resident Commissioner as a measure of enforced economy. By changing the nature of land-ownership in the country new classes were created and old traditional tribal rights were significantly undermined. This new class, a land-owning elite whose interests lay with the newly land-wealthy King, created the environment which would later produce a small loyal clique to bolster the Hashemite monarchy. The grace and favour of the tribes was maintained.

The second significant feature of this period was the creation, expansion and control of the Transjordanian military. Mention has previously been made of the establishment of the Arab Legion and the Transjordanian Frontier Force (TJFF). By 1929 the former was more akin to a police force in its duties and equipment than a regular army having been reduced from 1,300 to fewer than 900 in all ranks including a significant proportion of Palestinians and Syrians. This was because the TJFF, a polyglot imperial unit nominally part of the British army in Palestine, operated in Transjordan with responsibility for control of the desert and protection of the borders. However, due to such factors as low numbers of personnel and a small budget, it proved incapable of fulfilling this role in the face of increased cross-frontier tribal raiding. Accordingly, when Colonel (later General) John Bagot Glubb arrived in 1930 he became Peake's deputy but his main role was the formation and command of the Desert Patrol – a unit of 150 men equipped with armoured cars, modern weapons and wire-lesses. As he had previously done in Iraq, by 1932 Glubb had success-fully put an end to the tribal raiding. The desert patrol was nominally incorporated into the Arab Legion but was still under Glubb's command and the TJFF was withdrawn to Palestine to become part of the British mandate police force. From this point the Arab Legion resumed its original military role, with Glubb acting as an informal spokesman for the Bedouin tribes who provided the manpower for the Desert Patrol. As the Legion expanded to meet the requirements placed upon it by the Arab rebellion in Palestine of 1936–9 and the Second World War, Glubb ensured that the bulk of new recruitment for the expanding force came from the desert Bedouin. This gave the Legion and later the national army of Jordan, which was formed from it, the predominantly tribal background it still has today.

## ABDULLAH AND PALESTINE

The Emirate continued to develop steadily and for the most part peacefully throughout the 1930s. Emir Abdullah pursued his ambi-tions to play an international role, never letting go of his quest for control of a Greater Syria. As part of this process of expanding his area of influence, he attempted to involve himself in events in Palestine where the mandatory authorities were increasingly failing to satisfy the diametrically opposed demands of Arab and Jew during a period of increasing Jewish immigration. Inter-communal violence grew worse as more Jews fled to Palestine from Nazi persecution in Europe and both communities attacked the British for allegedly favouring the other. The Palestinians were reluctant to accept the Emir, an outsider and too close to the British, as their spokesman and his pretensions brought him into direct conflict with Haj Amin al-Husseini, the British appointed Grand Mufti of Jerusalem and who was from one of the most politically powerful Palestinian families. Abdullah then dramatically destroyed his credibility by having been exposed (together with some other East Bank landowners) as entering into covert and potentially highly profitable property deals with the Jewish Agency which was seeking land across the Jordan to embark on fresh colonies there. The Agency believed that 'the vast and empty lands across the river' had potential to assimilate many thousands of Jewish colonists and take off the pressure on scarcer land in more crowded Palestine (Gelber, 1997, p. 29). Hostile publicity in the Arab press frustrated these attempts to settle Jews in Transjordan, but the Agency kept up its attempts to find land until 1939.

When the Arab revolt in Palestine erupted in 1936, Abdullah sought to mediate between the various competing factions of the Palestinian leadership and between the Arab Higher Committee and the British. Once again the Palestinians who preferred to rely on more trustworthy intermediaries brushed him aside. This rejection of Abdullah was reinforced when it emerged that the Emir supported plans to partition Palestine as a last gasp attempt by the British to meet the aspirations of the two warring communities. The partition plan outlined by the Peel Commission was bitterly opposed by the Palestinian Arabs as a sell-out of their birthright. Abdullah had made a good impression on the Peel Commission when it visited Amman to solicit his views, but his lack of influence in Palestine made him little use as a mediator. When in July 1937 the Royal Commission formally proposed partition as a 'two state' solution, Abdullah confirmed the Palestinian Arabs, worst suspicions by announcing acceptance. It was hardly surprising that he did so as the Commission's report proposed that the Arab state should consist of Transjordan and the Arab part of Palestine. This was too tempting a prospect for Abdullah to let by, even though by his endorsement of the report's findings he completely isolated himself from the rest of Arab world and divided opinion in his own country. Subsequent changes of plans by the British in the face of unrelenting Arab hostility including the abandonment (for the moment) of partition, placing restrictions on Jewish immigration and other concessions to Arab opinion (some credited to Abdullah's influence) helped to restore his position within the Arab fold. The outbreak of the Second World War in 1939 effectively paralysed the Arab nationalist movement within Palestine and restored Abdullah's flickering hopes of successful foreign enterprises, including taking over the leadership of the Palestinian nationalists.

Abdullah's public support for British policy brought domestic benefits. He had an increase in his civil list (to £18,000); a decrease in financial and administrative supervision and the agreement to replace seconded foreign officials with Transjordanians where possible. The 1928 Organic Law was amended to replace the Executive Council with a Cabinet of ministers in charge of individual departments. His status was also given a boost by being authorised to appoint consular representatives to some neighbouring Arab countries.

## THE SECOND WORLD WAR AND THE ESTABLISHMENT OF ISRAEL

As an ally of Britain, Transjordan was one of the first countries to declare war on Germany. The Emirate never wavered in its support throughout the conflict, even after German successes in North Africa in 1941 when the British cause appeared lost in the Middle East. Later that year the Arab Legion fought with distinction alongside other allied troops in over-throwing the pro-Nazi Rashid Ali regime in Baghdad and helping to defeat the Vichy French in Syria. Battle experience in this conflict stood the Arab Legion in good stead for the subsequent hostilities with the infant Israeli State in 1948. By the end of the war it was at four times its pre-war strength and 7,400 in total, divided into three mechanised regiments and 16 infantry companies. The Arab Legion remained a mainly British officered force and there was little effective opposition within the country to Abdullah's pro-British policy. According to Wilson the British Resident in Amman exercised even more control over Transjordanian affairs than was explicitly indicated in the Anglo-Transjordanian treaty (Wilson, 1987, p. 130). Much of this was due to the personal friendship between the formidable and influential Resident Sir Alec Kirkbride and the Emir, whose interests in domestic matters (although not external) generally coincided (Kirkbride, 1976). In addition the Anglophile Emir was to form a strong friendship and rely on the advice of Gen. Glubb Pasha.

Throughout the war Emir Abdullah never lost sight of his ambitions to rule a Greater Syria which ideally would comprise Syria, Lebanon, Transjordan and Palestine. He also dreamed of adding Iraq through a federal arrangement to this Hashemite Empire. He accordingly attempted to build up a monarchist constituency after the overthrow of the Vichy French through bribery and propaganda – although many of his target audience amongst the Syrian nationalists may have preferred an Iraqi candidate such as the Regent Abd-al Illah or the young King Feisal from the other Hashemite branch of the family based in Baghdad. To have

Abdullah as their King seemed like replacing French hegemony with indirect British control as they already exercised in Amman. He also kept his hand in the Palestinian pot, encouraged by the exiling of the main leadership including the Mufti of Jerusalem Husseini following the ending of the Arab rebellion in 1939. But he failed to organise a strong body of political support. He was also rebuffed by the Jewish Agency in his attempts to get Zionist backing for his Greater Syrian enterprise in return for autonomy and a greater area for settlement than envisaged by partition. The Zionists were now pushing for a Jewish Commonwealth, unrestricted immigration and a rejection of the 1939 White Paper which had restricted such immigration and had optimistically (and unrealistically) foreshadowed a Palestinian government within ten years, subject to an accommodation between Jews and Arabs.

Transjordan had also been active towards the end of the war on a wider Arab stage. The emirate had taken part in discussions about the formation of the League of Arab States (The Arab League). This organisation came into being in March 1945 and besides Transjordan its original membership was composed of Egypt, Syria, Lebanon, Saudi Arabia, Iraq and Yemen. Its original purpose was partly to provide a framework for the old vision of a unified Arab state, but it never moved beyond an association of independent Arab states 'without any real unifying principle other than opposition to a Jewish State' (Rinehart, 1980, p. 24). This was particularly disappointing to Abdullah who was against any organisation which implied recognition of the existing divisions in the Arab world, diluting his vision of a united Fertile Crescent and he later described the League as 'seven heads thrust into a sack' (Sayegh, 1958, p. 121). Moreover the negotiations which led to the establishment of the Arab League revealed Transjordanian lack of clout, as compared with its Hashemite cousins in Iraq and their main rival for leadership in the Arab world – the Farouk monarchy in Egypt. Post-Vichy Syria seemed inclined to gravitate towards Cairo for protection against Abdullah's monarchist ambitions. Saudi Arabia also sided with Egypt against old Hashemite enemies, and the Lebanese were more at home with the cosmopolitan Egyptians than the more socially conservative desert societies. Abdullah's isolation from his fellow leaders was seen as the final nail in the coffin of his dreams of leading a Greater Syria.

Thus by the end of the war Abdullah, having failed to reach his Holy Grail of an expanded Hashemite empire, concentrated his efforts on achieving full independence. Here he was pushing at an open door once the hostilities were over, despite worries in some British quarters that real and visible independence for Transjordan would lead to agitation in Palestine for similar treatment for the Arabs there. By March 1946 a Treaty of 'perpetual peace and friendship' had been signed between the two countries. Transjordan became a Kingdom. To Abdullah's relief the British subsidy continued, including the financing of the Arab Legion – he had an agreement with his Iraqi cousins for them to pick up the tab if Britain used independence as a pretext for refusing to continue to pay up. So Transjordan continued to be financially and militarily dependent on Britain. The British military presence in the Kingdom was safeguarded in an annex to the treaty. This indication of continued British influence cast doubts on the real nature of Transjordan's independence, and both the United States and the Soviet Union withheld recognition-the Soviets blocked Transjordan's application for UN membership until 1948. The US did so under pressure from the Zionist lobby who urged the administration not to recognise an independent Transjordan until the future of Palestine had been established. The Syrians also regarded the military annex as inconsistent with full independence but were not too dismayed as the controversy over the annex and Abdullah's continued dependence on Britain was another – probably fatal – blow to his case for the Syrian throne. Abdullah crowned himself King on 25 May 1946, 23 years to the day that as Emir Abdullah he had proclaimed Transjordan as an 'independent part of the Arab Kingdom'. Whatever the Syrians and other Arabs might have thought, Abdullah's ambitions for a larger role in the region remained intact. When opening Parliament (as the Legislative Assembly was renamed in 1946) he called for unity between Transjordan and Syria. He also used his Legation in Damascus to distribute propaganda on his ideas for a Greater Syrian monarchy (Wilson, 1987, p. 158).

The end of the war also initiated another turbulent period for Palestine. In July 1945 the British Foreign Secretary ordered the implementation of the 1939 White paper. The limitation on Jewish immigration (to 75,000 a year) infuriated the Zionists, particularly in the aftermath of the exposure of the full horror of the Holocaust. Palestine became an area of conflict with Jewish guerrilla groups (many of whose members had served with the British Army in the war) carrying out acts of terrorism against mandate rule. Reprisals and counter-reprisals between Jews and Arabs and by both communities against the British increased. The British, exhausted and war weary, decided to toss this intractable problem into the lap of the UN. In response the General Assembly established the UN Special Committee on Palestine (UNSCOP), which in August 1947 proposed a complex system of partition into separate Arab and Jewish states, a special international status (*corpus separatum*) for a greater Jerusalem including Bethlehem and an economic union linking the three constituent parts.

Abdullah, who had welcomed the British proposal for partition when first proposed in 1937, was now more cautious in his public pronouncements although he had quietly advocated this solution to both the British and the Americans (whom the British now wanted to involve), as well as to the Jewish Agency since the end of the war. He continued to be in constant touch with the Agency and on occasions passing on to them his information on British policies and intentions on Palestine and demanding handouts of cash for his pains (Gelber, 1997, p. 195). He also entered into a secret agreement with the Jewish leadership not to let the Arab Legion enter into the territory of a Jewish State following the implementation of partition. The Americans quickly discovered that Abdullah's real intention was to use partition to expand his own domain (Wilson, 1987, p. 162). He even continued to hope that the Zionists might somehow help with the Greater Syrian project. Other Arab states and the Palestinians continued to oppose the division of Palestine. In the event the General Assembly accepted the UNSCOP recommendation to partition Palestine. The British abstained in the vote and subsequently announced its decision to evacuate Palestine and to terminate its administration on 15 May 1948.

Palestine soon became a cockpit for Arab-Jewish hostilities with fighting erupting even before the formal British withdrawal, with Jewish forces being particularly successful in establishing control over large areas of the country. As part of what was to become a campaign of deliberate ethnic cleansing, a massacre of villagers at Deir Yassin by Jewish *Irgun* irregulars set off an exodus of panic-stricken Palestinian refugees. Although the British initially attempted to keep the Arab Legion (with its British officers) out of the fighting, and although Abdullah and the Jewish Agency kept closely in touch over the possibility of Transjordan not being sucked into the growing conflict, this did not prove possible. On the instructions of the nearby Arab countries, Arab armies – or at least badly equipped, trained and led units representing Egypt, Syria and Iraq plus the ineffectual, ramshackle Arab Liberation Army together with the Arab Legion (which had been pulled back east of the Jordan by 14 May) invaded Palestine on 15 May. All units were under the nominal command of Abdullah in a vain attempt to recreate the successful fervour of the 1916 Hashemite-led Arab Revolt, except for the Legion which acted independently of Transjordanian command. In the ensuing conflict only the Arab Legion proved capable of standing up to the superior, more committed, better led Jewish troops defending and expanding the newly proclaimed State of Israel. By the time major hostilities ended in July 1948 most of the Arab armies had been expelled from their areas of operation by the Israelis except for the Arab Legion, which had successfully occupied and defended the Old City of Jerusalem (including the principal Muslim holy places). The Legion also occupied Hebron to the south and much of Samaria to the north. The Egyptians held on to Gaza. The subsequent cease-fire and Armistices eventually established a tacit acceptance of the military boundaries as the status quo.

In all this Abdullah adhered to his secret understanding with the Jewish Agency not to enter any territory allocated to the Jewish State by the UN. This virtue was made a necessity by the British stricture that British officers in the Legion were not allowed to fight inside the 'Jewish areas'. Despite losing some territory to the Israelis, notably the towns of Lydda and Ramla, in a subsequent round of fighting (in which British troops stood ready to defend Aqaba against the Israelis in accordance with their 1946 Treaty obligations) Abdullah, through the success of the Arab Legion, had legitimised and realised his expansionist ambitions in Palestine. Arab suspicions of continued collusion with the Israelis notwithstanding (despite bitter and prolonged fighting between the Arab Legion and Jewish troops) Abdullah could present himself as the only effective defender of the Palestinians – some of whose leaders had *in extremis* invited his assistance believing that they had no alternative. In general his stock in Palestinian eyes had sharply tumbled after the loss of Lydda and Ramla.

## THE HASHEMITE KINDOM AND THE DEATH OF ABDULLAH

Despite strong hostility from the other Arab states in opposing any recognition of the status quo, Abdullah moved to consolidate his military gains. He showed a disposition to accept the cease-fire boundaries as the legitimate frontiers of his expanded kingdom. Led by Egypt, which established an Arab government for Palestine in Gaza, the Arab League members opposed any partition of Palestine and Abdullah's gain thereby (Wilson, 1987, p. 177).

Abdullah's retort was to proclaim himself as King of All Palestine at a well-attended and skilfully orchestrated conference in the West Bank town of Jericho in December 1949. Here the King strove to create the impression that he had widespread popular Palestinian support for his act of union. He subsequently formally annexed the territory he held on 29 April 1950. A resolution to unite both banks of the river Jordan (East and West) was introduced into parliament by a group of Palestinian deputies and was passed unanimously. This act was recognised by Britain three days later. This annexation followed elections held on both sides of the Jordan. In the meantime the country's name was changed to the Hashemite Kingdom of Jordan and three Palestinians were included in the cabinet. Abdullah's position was salvaged from complete isolation when in late 1948 all Arab countries (including Jordan) that had been involved in the fighting signed armistices. On 31 January 1949 the US at last recognised Jordan as an independent country.

For the rest of King Abdullah's reign his Hashemite Kingdom remained politically isolated in the Arab world as represented by the Arab League. The League fell short of expelling Jordan when the King refused to issue a statement that the annexation of the West Bank (as that part of Palestine occupied by the Jordanians and subsequently by the Israelis post-1967 came to be called) was only temporary. The Arab states were anxious to retain the principle that there was a state called Palestine whose Arab inhabitants had rights to independence and sovereignty under Palestinian not Jordanian rule. They feared (with some justice) that Abdullah could only hold on to West Bank with the acquiescence of the Israelis, thus breaking Arab ranks and further depriving the Palestinians of much of their birth right in virtual collaboration with the Zionist enemy. Abdullah had also kept wounds open by restating his Greater Syrian ambitions at the opening of the new Jordanian parliament. On the wider international stage Jordan drifted away from the Arab League by, for example, supporting UN (and therefore US) policy over Korea and signing an agreement with the US in 1951 (Lawless, 1998, p. 630).

Although, as discussed in chapter four, Jordan's fairly bleak long term economic prospects were enhanced by the annexation of the comparatively developed and more agriculturally productive West Bank, the country faced an enormous task in absorbing the refugees who had fled or had been driven out from what was now Israel. By May 1949 the total numbers of refugees on relief in Transjordan and Arab Palestine was just over half a million. Further expulsions from Israel had now slowed if not yet stopped. Of these 100,000 were in Jordan 'proper' and the rest on the West Bank – thus doubling the previous population of the Arab West Bank. An influx into Amman had increased the population of the capital from 50,000 in early 1948 to 120,000 by October 1950. From its formation in May 1950 the UN Relief and Works Agency (UNRWA) took over from the UN Disaster Relief Fund the task of looking after the Palestinian refugees. On the constitutional front a further agreement with Britain in March 1948 had removed the intrusive provisions of the 1946 independence treaty. All restrictions on sovereignty were removed although limited British base and transit rights in Jordan continued, as did the British subsidy that paid for the Arab legion.

King Abdullah did not live long to enjoy his expanded domains. He had made numerous enemies as a result of his policies in late 1940s. Not exclusively because of his relationship with the Jewish authorities before and after the foundation of Israel, but also because of his ambitions for a Hashemite led Greater Syria dominating the Fertile Crescent – Syria, Transjordan and Palestine to be joined in confederation by Hashemite Iraq. Several plots and conspiracies to assassinate the King surfaced or were exposed in 1949 and eventually on 25 July 1951 a single gunman shot him down (nearly killing his grandson Hussein as well) at the entrance of the Al Aqsa Mosque in Jerusalem (Gelber, 1997, p. 289). It is argued by some that it was to the credit of the stability which Abdullah had created in the young Jordanian state in troubled times that the crown passed to his eldest son Talal with no visible indications of dissent. Yet others have argued that so autocratic was Abdullah's rule and so bereft of political opportunity was the majority of the population that it was inevitable that the succession was achieved so smoothly. The immediate aftermath of the succession, however, could not be described as stable in any way.

Hastily arranged trials for a group of 'assassins' associated with the killer (who had himself been shot dead by Abdullah's guards) led to the speedy trial of ten men and the subsequent execution of four. One theory places the responsibility for the choreography of the trial and rapid executions on to Sir Alec Kirkbride, the still influential British Ambassador in Amman, who believed that public safety required getting the judicial proceedings out of the way as rapidly as possible (Wilson,

1987, p. 212). Probably deliberately so as not to enflame passions the alleged motives of the plotters were not explored in depth – although a link was popularly believed to have existed with Abdullah's old adversary Haj Amin al Husseini. His cousin Musa al Husseini was one of the accused (Kirkbride, 1976, p. 137). Accordingly the real motivations of the assassin and accomplices remain unclear to this day, although Abdullah's collusion with the Israelis to the detriment of the Palestinians was held at that time to be the most likely motive.

So Abdullah died with his ambitions for a much greater kingdom unfulfilled. The West Bank was little compensation for the entire Fertile Crescent. His monument was, however, to be the creation of the basis for the modern Hashemite Kingdom, which with admittedly considerable British assistance, he had carved out of an insignificant patch of real estate which no-one seemed to want nor knew what to do with. And ironically given his expansionist ambitions a Kingdom which as a result of the 1967 war was to contract to within the boundaries that Abdullah had reluctantly (if only temporally) accepted in the 1920s.

# Chapter 2

## CONTEMPORARY POLITICS IN JORDAN

The assassination of King Abdullah had significant implications for the stability of the Hashemite kingdom and its development as a nation. Domestic politics throughout the 1950s would be characterised by immense change, upheaval and eventually severe restrictions imposed on all aspects of political life by the country's new monarch Hussein. The chaotic and unpredictable circumstances of Abdullah's death, the near assassination of his grandson Hussein beside him and the instability within royal circles following a short-lived stab at rule by Hussein's father Talal contributed to a severe crisis of confidence both inside and outside the kingdom over the ability of the Hashemites to rule and retain their legitimacy. Indeed, Abdullah's assassination could not have come at a worse time. Under British tutelage Abdullah had concentrated political power into his own hands and the fragile kingdom had been shaken by war with Israel, while the influx of a sizeable refugee population and a regional environment predicated revolutionary change. The only significant political event to occur under the short-lived rule of King Talal was the establishment of a new constitution for the country in 1952. The constitution was an important guideline to the outline of state and system of government at a time when the very foundations of the Jordanian State had been shaken by Abdullah's death.

Important insights into the nature of state and government can be garnered from the 1952 Constitution. In many ways the new constitution mirrored the provisions of Abdullah's 1928 Organic Law (Abu Nowar, 1989, pp. 291–299). The role of religion, or more specifically Islam, is emphasised. Islam is again characterised as the religion of the state but is now set within the context of a parliamentary system of government with a hereditary monarchy. As in 1928, the judicial system has a dual nature with provision for Shari'a courts alongside civil and special courts. The constitution re-endorses the authority of the Shari'a courts on all matters of personal status in the kingdom affecting its majority Muslim population, whilst preserving the rights of non-Muslims. The most important provisions of the new constitution were those establishing a parliamentary form of government, much advanced from the simple neocolonial measures in the 1928 Organic law. This was to be a bi-cameral legislature with many features of other modern parliamentary systems of that time, for example an elected chamber of deputies (broadly based male adult franchise) and an appointed upper chamber or Senate. The lower chamber could force the resignation of individual ministers (by impeachment) or the entire government through a vote of confidence. The assent of both chambers was necessary for the passing of legislation, which was subject to possible amendment by both houses.

The accession of Abdullah's grandson Hussein to the throne in 1953 at the age of eighteen did not augur well for the future. Not only did the young King have to establish himself as a credible and capable leader, he would also have to withstand the dual pressures of British and Arab opinion. Moreover he was required to preside over a kingdom which was host to a large refugee population, had announced a new constitution, annexed territory to the West of its borders and was seeking to establish itself during the opening episodes of popular Arab nationalism, various regional movements for independence and the Cold War. Indeed, from 1953–1957 as the new monarch wrestled with the immense task not only of leadership but also of rule, the forces of the Arab left prepared to mount their most significant challenge ever to Hashemite rule.

The forces of the left saw Abdullah's departure as a 'window of opportunity' for pushing and securing their radical republican programme. These radical parties, which included the socialist Ba'ath, mainly reflected the aspirations of those Palestinians who had settled in the country following the war of 1948–49. They had lived unhappily with Abdullah's claims to Jerusalem, his control of West Bank territory and his contacts with the new Jewish state and believed his demise to be an important catalyst in their quest for power. They gambled on the inability of the new monarch – young, inexperienced and western educated – to meet the challenge mounted by the left in Jordan and supported by the call of radical Arab nationalism echoing through the region. They quickly set about questioning a number of aspects of Hashemite rule, in particular the continued British presence in the political and especially military affairs of the country at a time when the movement for Arab national independence and anti-colonialism was at its zenith.

As a result of the activities of radical agitators, the authority of the government, headed by its young King, was threatened and under-mined by a series of riots, demonstrations and political protests.

Indeed, for three years the monarch seemed to limp from one serious problem to another: from Bangdung to the Baghdad Pact, the Eisenhower doctrine to Suez. Rumours of imminent revolutionary change gripped the country, as the new King barely coped with a series of crises. Governments changed in rapid succession. Even hitherto loyal political forces, such as the conservative Islamic movement – the Muslim Brotherhood – engaged in protests against the Baghdad Pact in 1955 as yet another administration fell and further demonstrations spread through the country.

In response the King attempted a policy of appeasement to local pressure. For example, in 1956 he ordered the British commander of the Jordanian army, Glubb Pasha, together with most British officers, out of the country. But the left sought only to further undermine Hashemite rule. Spurred on or encouraged by events in Iraq where the future of Hashemite monarch Feisal, Hussein's cousin, looked precarious to say the least, the situation in Jordan further deteriorated in 1956 and in 1957. And following the US administration's promulgation of the Eisenhower doctrine, the King faced further political unrest, an attempted coup and subsequently elections which returned a left-leaning government led by Sulaiman Nablusi.

The King's response to this challenge in 1957 proved to be an important turning point in the political life of the country for a variety of reasons. Not least because in order to retain power and assert his authority, the King embarked on a series of policies or actions which would signal the end of any attempt at constitutional rule. As Salibi notes, ultimately 'democracy was sacrificed for stability until further notice and no pretence was made to the contrary' (Salibi, 1993, p. 203). Indeed most aspects of political life in the country were suspended as the King announced that political parties would be banned, full elections suspended and the Nablusi government dismissed. The legislative functions of the lower house of Parliament were rarely utilised (other than to rubber stamp decisions from the monarch), and the King as he grew in confidence further concentrated political power into his hands. He exerted his authority over the army again, purging it of the elements behind the attempted coup, political opponents were arrested and imprisoned by the King's burgeoning internal security structure (*Mukhabaraat*), the press was brought under control and the media placed in the King's hands.

From this point onwards real political power and authority in the country became the preserve of the few rather than the many. All aspects of constitutional politics and democracy went into decline as the power of the King, court and notable families increased out of all proportion to their numbers. Indeed, the King himself was by no means averse to amending aspects of the 1952 constitution to further enhance executive authority in the country. In 1958, for example, article 33 of the constitution was amended to allow the King authority to declare war, conclude peace and ratify any treaties and agreements. In addition, after 1957, as Mutawi has noted, King Hussein's influence over policy formulation in domestic affairs grew considerably, (Mutawi, 1987, p. 3) while his grip on the military and foreign policy making was further bolstered. The impact of this realignment of power on the formal mechanisms of government, as stipulated and outlined by the constitution, was quickly apparent as after 1957 the legislature and cabinet assumed a subordinate, emasculated and virtually advisory function.

The events of the mid-1950s combined with the ability of the King to use the power entitled to him under the terms of the constitution effectively ended hopes for real people-based participatory politics in the country. Franchise, limited rather than universal, became meaningless in a political environment where elected representatives had no real power to formulate policies within the kingdom. Indeed, even the 'influence' of parliament and its elected representatives was frustrated by the growing stature and importance of the new elite-based powerhouse of Jordanian politics – the royal court or diwan.

The diwan in Jordan is not a unique feature of the political landscape of the Middle East; rather it is representative of states based on monarchical or dynastic rule such as Saudi Arabia or Kuwait. In Jordan the Royal Hashemite Diwan or Royal Court fulfils a variety of functions and is populated by a stratified elite including members of the extended Hashemite dynasty itself, notable families and tribal leaders. The Diwan has been described as 'as influential as the Cabinet … [and] as an executive council in a vital sector of domestic politics, (Mutawi, 1987, p. 12). In the latter years of King Hussein's life, the Royal Court grew as a reflection of the King's personal authority. He called most of the shots, often acting behind a facade of a superficially empowered Prime Minister. In addition there can be little doubt that the legitimacy of the regime in Jordan after 1957 was inextricably tied up with the role of this local elite and the important base of support it created for the young king. Of course, the rewards for such loyalty were important and it is this circle, along with the Cabinet, which enjoyed the financial benefits and social status associated with the exalted status of the Royal Court. What should not be underestimated in an assessment of the role of the Diwan is the important legitimating function it can fulfil in a country like Jordan. With a small population, limited territory and notions of national identity constructed around the theme of tribe, family and clan the officials of the Diwan were able to represent the monarch's policy directly back to their localised spheres of power and use this in turn to keep the King in touch with the 'grassroots'. Indeed, the late King Hussein was almost literally able to embrace the Hashemite nation by personally receiving all visitors to the Royal Court and by frequent visits to all parts of his realm. As King Hussein grew in political stature and authority the importance of individuals within the Royal Court declined and by the 1990s they were on the whole courtiers rather than influential advisers. The Diwan also served the useful purpose of absorbing senior politicians (or fringe members of the Hashemite family) whose political shelf life had expired and who could enjoy a well deserved semi-retirement in an important sounding position but with no real authority.

The other institution of state, which the King became increasingly dependent on after 1957, was the army. Like the Diwan, the Jordanian Army – the Arab Legion – is intimately associated and tied to the monarch rather than the state per se. The army in Jordan has been utilised by the King in a variety of functions. Of course the formal provisions of the 1952 constitution declare the King supreme commander of land, naval and air forces. In addition, as previously mentioned only the King is empowered to declare war, sue for peace etc. Only the King can declare martial law and bring the army onto the streets within the country. In addition to this formal provision the linkage between monarch and army has been at the bedrock of the state since its inception. No wonder then that the British attached so much importance to the army and influence within it until the dismissal of Glubb Pasha and other British officers in 1956.

Following the final departure of the remaining British forces in 1958 King Hussein – often referred to as a monarch in uniform (which he usually wore on formal occasions) – reasserted his personal authority over the armed forces. In addition members of the royal family had key positions in the Bedouin-based national army. The military in a country like Jordan could help build the nation, just as the Hashemites had built the Jordanian kingdom on the force and loyalty of the Arab revolt and loyal Bedouin soldiers. The military has long had a social development role with its teaching hospital (King Hussein Medical Centre) and its running of schools in rural areas. From Glubb's time young Jordanians were sent on military scholarships to the UK and elsewhere to learn medicine, engineering and other professional skills which they practised in uniform.

As one author argues: 'If freewheeling democracy had to be sacrificed, temporarily, to the exigencies of building a nation and transforming an economy, that appeared an acceptable price to pay'. Or as Ralph Halpern declared in his book, *The Politics of Social Change in the Middle East*, 'the military is the vanguard of society, it embodies the hopes and objectives of the new professional middle class ... and will act as a revolutionary force in Middle Eastern society' (p. 274). From King Hussein's perspective, and this is equally likely to apply to the new monarch with his own military background, the Jordanian Arab Legion has almost a mystical position at the heart and soul of the Jordanian nation. It was frequently referred to as such by King Hussein and senior military commanders. The late King often portrayed it at the natural lineal successor to the 'Arab army' who had fought at his great grandfather's behest in the Great Arab Revolt of 1916. This rhetoric and myth creation reflected an important plank in the platform of legitimacy invoked by the Hashemites as rulers of modern Jordan.

Thus, by the end of the 1950s the political climate in Jordan had been transformed. While at the beginning of the decade a new constitution had enshrined an array of political rights and freedoms to the citizens of the state, the new monarch feeling himself under pressure set about limiting, suspending and amending such rights. By the close of the decade political parties had been banned, parliament suspended, the King had increased his own powers and the army played an increasingly important role in the internal arena. For the new King, in the face of strong radical opposition, stability could only be ensured through coercion, severe restrictions on democratic life in the country and allegiance through traditional primordial appeals to religion, tribe, clan and family. The forces of radical Arab nationalism were rigorously resisted as the King created a conservative political environment and became increasingly dependent on western financial support.

Domestic politics in Jordan throughout the 1960s were limited to say the least. King Hussein, now confident of his iron grip, depended increasingly on the army rather than the constitution. Indeed any semblance of constitutional politics in the country was sorely lacking and Hussein's opposition was increasingly forced underground as the wounds from the battles of 1957 were licked. Nevertheless, as the decade progressed the environment of Arab radicalism that now characterised the region slowly but surely permeated the ranks of Jordan's activist strata. In addition, as King Hussein found himself under increasing pressure from Nasser of Egypt to up the military ante with Israel, the political environment in the country became increasingly tense and popular support grew for taking on the Israelis. Domestic considerations, including an already large Palestinian refugee community within his own borders, made it extremely difficult for King Hussein to resist Nasser's calls to strike against Israel. Goaded into siding with Nasser and the Syrians in June 1967 King Hussein was forced very much against his better judgement to order his troops to prepare for conflict with Israel. As he knew it would be, the consequences of the Six-Day War were devastating for the Jordanian regime. The Jordanian army proved inadequate in battle and was not supported by their allies, and ceded territory to Israel within a few hours of joining in the hostilities. By the end of the war, Jordan had lost the West Bank and Arab East Jerusalem to Israel, thousands of refugees fled into the country and Arab military prestige was in tatters. King Hussein was humiliated; he had been forced to participate in a war he wanted no part of and had lost half a kingdom into the bargain.

As King Hussein and his government turned their attention inward again the scene that greeted them in the truncated kingdom of the East Bank of the Jordan was threatening to say the least. When the Palestinian resistance network in the West Bank was destroyed during the war the PLO, Fatah and its other constituent associations needed a new base for its activities. Thus, along with the swell of Palestinian refugees crossing from the West to the East Bank, the PLO and its fedayeen fighters began the process of transfer to Jordan. Throughout 1968 it became increasingly apparent that the fedayeen would maintain the pressure on Israel as they organised one raid after another against Jewish targets. While King Hussein did little to hinder the PLO and their fighters he grew increasingly uneasy at the growing numbers of Palestinians armed by the movement. The King, in an attempt to maintain control over his country, maintained martial law, which had been introduced during the war with Israel. Yet martial law did little to insulate the Kingdom from the effects of PLO activities within their own borders and beyond.

The internal situation, however, was significantly altered by the events of 1968 and in particular the Battle of Karameh. The early months of 1968 had been characterised by numerous guerrilla raids across the river Jordan on Israel; casualties were high and the government in Tel Aviv decided to attack the PLO back on Jordanian territory. With advance notice of Israeli intentions, the PLO and Jordanian army met to decide a strategy – the meetings highlighted disparate views and tensions both within the Palestinian camp and between Fatah and the Jordanian army. Nevertheless, when an Israeli armoured group invaded the Jordanian town of Karameh on 21 March Palestinian fighters and Jordanian soldiers stood shoulder to shoulder in battle against Israel. Thanks mainly to the counter offensive led by Jordanian tanks the Israelis were compelled to withdraw with heavy casualties. The Jordanian army acquitted itself well and made a good job of exploiting Israeli military over-confidence. Within the Arab world, however, PLO propagandists from Cairo to Baghdad promoted accounts of the daring feats of Palestinian bravery and resistance. Indeed, as Sayigh notes: 'Astute manipulation of the media by the guerrillas left many Jordanian officers and soldiers with the feeling that their hard-earned victory had been stolen by upstarts, and inserted a sour note into relations that was to grow into deep bitterness over the next two years' (Sayigh, 1997, p. 179). The Jordanians were thus denied international recognition of their victory, although it was said that because of the Arab army's performance at Karameh they earned the grudging respect of Israeli generals for many years to come.

King Hussein became increasingly concerned at the situation for a number of reasons. The first issue of concern was the increasing size, swagger and confidence of the fedayeen movement in Jordan. By the end of the 1960s Palestinian guerrillas moved openly and freely around the entire country, their arms on open public display. Secondly, the battle of Karameh had created, within the Arab world, a perception of success for the guerrillas, which dangerously ignored the Jordanian dimension. Finally, the Jordanian army grew increasingly annoyed and discontented at the growing military profile of the PLO's guerrillas and the internal threat they posed. This last factor was particularly important for a king like Hussein, whose legitimacy and future was inextricably tied to the Jordanian military. If the Jordanian army could not maintain internal security, what were the consequences for the national security of the country?

## CIVIL WAR

In the early 1970s one event and one event alone shaped internal politics in Jordan – the brief civil war which took place between King Hussein's armed forces and the Palestinian population led by the PLO. It was during this period that the future of the Kingdom and not just its monarchy reached a point of precariousness that shook the notion of the Hashemite nation, territoriality and its existence to the core. The term Black September, while later referring to a Palestinian guerrilla group formed after 1970, is used, particularily by Palestinians, to mark the events that led King Hussein's army to battle with the PLO and the subsequent defeat and expulsion of Yasser Arafat and his followers. By contrast, to many East Bankers who revelled in the Palestinian defeat at the hands of the Jordanian army it is known as 'White September'.

While it was evident to King Hussein when he assumed the throne in 1953 that the national make up in Jordan would always have a Palestinian element the events of the late 1950s had led the monarch and his supporters to believe that the Palestinian issue could be contained, albeit with some difficulty. In many respects this policy of containment reflected the prevailing Arab attitude to the Palestinian issue and was no different from that advocated in Cairo or Damascus. Arab leaders like Hussein and Nasser believed that Palestinian interests were best served by co-ordinated Arab direction and not by independent action by the Palestinian leadership.

The events of 1967, however, as we have outlined above, irrevocably undermined the Arab claim to champion the Palestinian cause. The same crisis of confidence in Arab nationalist rhetoric now found its voice in the alleys of Cairo and was echoed in the streets of Amman, the refugee camps and the ghettos of the hundreds of thousands of Palestinians who now resided in the country. As Jordan endured a second refugee wave, the debilitating and humiliating loss of the West Bank including control of Arab East Jerusalem and it holy sites only added to a deep sense of humiliation in the Hashemite camp. Not only in Jordan but also throughout the Arab world people looked for scapegoats to blame for their disastrous showing against the Israeli enemy.

In many respects, however, the tribulations of 1967, traumatic as they were as seen from a Jordanian perspective, would pale in comparison to the events in 1970s when Jordanians found themselves confronted by the Palestinians. Indeed, as Salibi notes, by 'October

1970, the very survival of Jordan as a state appeared to be at stake' (Salibi, 1993, p. 239). With fedayeen bases established in Jordan King Hussein had to contend with an enlarged refugee population from territory outside his own East Bank borders and with a population that was heavily armed and included personnel who were able to quickly establish a quasi-state infrastructure within his sovereign territory. Not only was the PLO able to create a 'state within a state' but more importantly for the survival of the Hashemite monarchy, the Palestinians were prepared to challenge the very legitimacy of the state which had provided shelter to hundreds of thousands of their people. In addition the King was becoming increasingly concerned about the ferocity of Israeli reprisals against Jordanians and not Palestinians for PLO raids into Israel. This was a deliberate Israeli policy in an attempt to force the King to tighten his grip on the PLO but in some respects, as we shall see, this policy also threatened the maintenance of the very same *status quo* in Jordan which it was in Israel's interest to preserve.

The events, which preceded the Black September conflict, were marked by increasing tension in the relationship between King Hussein's regime and the fedayeen movement headed by the PLO. While the regime had been aware of the threat posed by yet another large influx of refugees and radicalisation of the Palestinian issue at a regional level its policies of containment were resisted at every level. In the wake of the war the Palestinians blamed Jordan for their predicament and derided the King's army. Criticism of the poor performance of the Arab Legion in the war struck at the heart of the regime and was considered a personal insult to the King's ability to govern effectively. Adding insult to injury many Palestinians in the radical left including the PFLP (Popular Front for the Liberation of Palestine) 'called for the overthrow of the Arab monarchies, including the Hashemite regime in Jordan, arguing that this was an essential first step toward the liberation of Palestine' (Gerner, 1994, p. 121). King Hussein, however, was not willing to tolerate this threat to his authority, nor the argument that the route to liberation of Jerusalem led first through the streets of Amman.

The ability of Hussein and his leadership to re-assert their authority over the Palestinian population became crucial. What became clear was that a resort to legislative or constitutional measures would not be enough to contain the threat. While martial law had been declared in 1967 as a means by which the coercive arm of the state could be given greater freedom and authority to deal with the threat, this had done little to repress the growing strength of Palestinian nationalism as constituted within Jordan's borders. Indeed recourse to such measures reflected the growing crisis of confidence within the Hashemite regime as shown by the desperate steps they were prepared to take in the face of the Palestinian threat on their own doorstep. In addition the agreement of November 1968 between Jordan and the PLO which was supposed to keep relations cordial and free from tension grew increasingly irrelevant as fedayeen attacks on Israeli territory were maintained as a matter of priority by the Palestinians. This was in complete disregard of previous agreements with the Jordanian authorities.

By late 1969 and early 1970 the prospect of a serious military engagement between Jordan and the Palestinians appeared inevitable as tensions grew on both sides. Palestinian confidence had been bolstered by the battle of Karameh and the ever increasing (if not particularily effective) military forays over Jordan's borders and into Israel. The King and his army grew more and more alarmed at the proliferation of fedayeen training camps, the increasingly large number of recruits to the Palestinian cause and the marginalisation of their role in this process. The PLO had virtually taken over Jordan, was training its own fighters and educating and providing welfare for its own large refugee community, while the official institutions of the Jordanian state were bypassed and effectively placed on the sidelines. A 'state within a state' had more or less been established. An attempt in February 1970 by the Jordanian government to restrict the powers of the PLO only 'worsened the situation' according to Lukacs, who notes that 'After the decree was issued, fighting erupted in Amman for two days. The fighting stopped once Hussein agreed to suspend the decree but the conflict between the two sides did not stop' (Lukacs, 1997, p. 112).

The turning point in the impending crisis came in the summer of 1970 when Arab support for the Palestinian cause appeared to be further eroded by the acceptance of both King Hussein and Nasser of Egypt of the American formulated Rogers' Plan which placed resolution of the Palestinian issue into spheres outside PLO control. The Palestinian response to the Rogers' plan was one of outright rejection and both Nasser and King Hussein were bitterly criticised by the PLO for pursuing and protecting their own interests at the expense of the Palestinian people. The sense of abandonment within the Palestinian camp encouraged the radical leftist wing of the PLO and in particular the PFLP led by George Habash to argue convincingly that the time had come for Palestinians to go it alone and organise rebellion against the Hashemite leaders of Amman.

By this point, however, King Hussein and his supporters were ready to launch an offensive against the PLO. And after months of shoring up confidence in his army and among his Bedouin supporters Hussein ordered his troops to reassert its authority over the entire Kingdom and to defeat the guerrilla movement. King Hussein was not prepared to entertain in any way shape or form the much-touted duality of power sharing with the PLO, which jeopardised Jordanian sovereignty. But despite his determination to keep control the weeks following witnessed successive illustrations of the regime's weakening political grip over the country. The most dramatic incident was the Dawson's Field hi-jackings organised by the Popular Front for the Liberation of Palestine (PFLP) on September 6 which had caused considerable embarrassment to the government. The PFLP were able to hi-jack three aeroplanes belonging to Western airlines. Two of them were flown to Dawson's Field in northern Jordan controlled by the PFLP. The third was diverted to Cairo and blown up seconds after the passengers had been disembarked. Yet another airliner, a BOAC VC-10 full of school children, was also hi-jacked and flown to Dawson's Field where it and the other two aircraft were evacuated by the guerrillas and destroyed. All this whilst the Jordanian army looked on, unable to intervene. The three Western European governments involved (British, Germans and Swiss) were forced to negotiate with the PFLP to ensure the safety of their nationals, freeing a number of PFLP terrorists held in Europe including one who had failed to hi-jack an Israeli airliner.

According to Lukacs the 'hijacking, almost more than any other act, showed that the Jordanian army was vulnerable, and, thus, the seeds of an open confrontation began to germinate' (Lukacs, 1997, p. 112). This course to confrontation, notes Sayigh, was just what elements of the PFLP wanted to provoke with the hijackings, designed, therefore 'to disseminate a revolutionary atmosphere' ... Indeed Habash, the PFLP leader, deliberately sought to embroil the Palestinian movement in a general confrontation [with the Jordanian regime]' (Sayigh, 1997, p. 257). Habash along with other revolutionary Palestinians would mark short time before the confrontation they believed they would easily win against the Jordanian regime and its army.

On September 16,1970 King Hussein ordered his troops to strike against the fedayeen network and eliminate it as quickly as possible. Outnumbered, badly trained and often over-confident of their abilities, the Palestinian fighters, calling themselves the Palestine Liberation Army (PLA) under command of Arafat, proved unable to cope with this attack from the better armed and disciplined Jordanian Arab Army. This was despite Syrian support, including an attempted invasion from the north. The Iraqis, who had 12,000 men stationed inside Jordan, also found themselves embroiled but pulled out without firing a shot. The Syrian incursion in support of the PLO was turned back by Jordanian armour with a loss of more than half of their 200 tanks and (possibly) by the threat of Israeli involvement in support of Jordan.

Further Arab involvement was forthcoming by the end of September as Nasser and the Egyptians stepped in to apply pressure on both sides to halt conflict and negotiate a cease-fire. This pressure successfully resulted in a cease-fire by the beginning of October, but this was only a temporary respite. In the short-term the war left the PLO seriously weakened and the Jordanians had effectively curtailed the guerrilla movement. But despite this success, on the Jordanian side, the events of the September conflict were chalked up as nothing more than round one in the regime's confrontation with Palestinian nationalism. From October onwards the King regrouped his nation along with his army in preparation for the final showdown aimed at ousting the PLO from the kingdom. To achieve this the King appointed a new Prime Minster, Wasfi al-Tall, a tough East Bank nationalist and outspoken anti-Palestinian. As Salibi notes, 'In effect, Tall headed a war cabinet, intent from the very start on completing the liquidation of the fedayeen movement in Jordan. The surge of Jordanian patriotic feeling... provided the king and his new prime minister with firm backing for this policy' (Salibi, 1993, p. 239). The King was in no position to countenance an arrangement which permitted the PLO to continue undermining Hashemite rule; it was a question of Hashemite hegemony or nothing.

Through a thorough and unrelenting process of curtailing guerrilla activity, confining the PLO to the refugee camps, enforced disarmament, a heavy security crackdown and further limited skirmishes between the Jordanian army and Palestinian factions the tide turned against the PLO and its expulsion became a matter of when not if. By the summer of 1971 the Jordanians had effectively achieved their objectives; the PLO had been forced to leave Jordan and the last remaining guerrilla bases, including Ajlun, were overrun in further engagements. Arab attempts at mediation between King Hussein and Yasser Arafat proved fruitless as both sides formulated mutually opposing positions underpinned by intransigence. By November 1971 King Hussein ordered the final rout of the PLO as his government renewed martial law and closed down the two remaining PLO offices in Amman. The rupture was complete, and with it went the last vestiges of the Palestinian state-within-the-state in Jordan 'and the start of a new era of national consolidation of the Hashemite dynasty in this troubled territory (Sayigh, 1997, p. 281).

In many respects the events of 1970–1971 transformed the state-building task in Jordan, reshaped the debate about national identity and further limited the prospects of an early end to the increasingly authoritarian rule of the Hashemite oligarchy. National identity and nation took on new meanings within the kingdom as new symbols, histories of internal conflict and national narratives were reconstructed to account for the traumatic events of the post '67 period. While King Hussein had secured his position in the hearts and minds of his loyal East Bankers the remaining presence of a large Palestinian minority (on its way to becoming a majority) required new thinking within Jordanian circles. Distrust and continuing hostility towards the PLO were the principal factors which drove Hussein's Palestinian policy throughout the 1970s. This in turn created an atmosphere within the Kingdom in which hostility between Palestinian and Jordanian became an inescapable part of everyday life. While officially the Palestinian and East Bank populations were viewed as 'one nation', in practice the legacy of civil war resulted in a variety of informal practices of discrimination emerging from this period onwards. Martial law, for example, in the face of the Palestinian threat, was maintained and consistently used against large numbers of Palestinians who were routinely arrested and imprisoned without trial. The security services were charged with maintaining the King's authority and any hint of political dissent or opposition from within Palestinian circles was thoroughly investigated. In the public arena the appeal to Hashemite identity was broadcast through the state-controlled media, and the image of King and his national armed forces became a recurring motif found in one expression or another in every café, shop, hotel and many homes throughout the country.

## DOWNSIZING A KINGDOM

The early 1980s were characterised by relative stability within the country, largely due to the maintenance of martial law and an effective security crackdown. The suspension of constitutional politics did, however, lead to new forms of opposition emerging in the country. Political activists expressed discontent or an alternative voice in a variety of forums, but in particular in non-governmental organisations such as student movements, the Muslim Brotherhood and other Islamist bodies and professional associations such as those for engineers, doctors and pharmacists. In the absence of formal provisions for democracy, election to such associations was the only means of measuring the political state of play in the kingdom. In these forums a semblance of political life came to the fore, elections were hotly contested, particularly by activists from leftist factions within the country and Palestinians who could use these bodies to play a political role, no matter how minor, in the country. The activities of these non-governmental groups were contained by increasingly strict enforcement of the Kingdom's charities law – under which most of these groups were registered – and surveillance by Jordan's intelligence service, including infiltration by their agents of these associations and bodies. There was often nothing surreptitious about such monitoring. For example many organisations, including the most innocuous, had written into their rulebook the requirement that a member of the GID (General Intelligence Directorate-or *Mukhabaraat*) had to be present at the Annual General Meeting of the organisation before the proceedings could formally get under way. The Jordan-British Society still observes this requirement.

By the middle of the decade, however, as the share of wealth within the kingdom declined for the majority and increased for a minority, political tension increased. In 1986 serious demonstrations broke out at the University of Yarmouk, as students protesting a rise in university fees engaged in a pitched battle against the police and army. That same year the King introduced and Parliament approved a new electoral law. The new law was significant for a variety of reasons, not least because in theory it enfranchised women for the first time, and the number of deputies to the House of Representatives was raised from 60 to 142. In addition there would be further future allocation of seats along sectarian/ethnic/national lines, reserving seats in the parliament for refugees, Christians, Circassians and Chechens. (This was a refinement of the provisions of the 1928 Organic Law). Many

Jordanians, however, questioned the usefulness of a new electoral law when political parties were still banned and full-elections had not been held in the country since the late 1950s. The legislation, did, however, prove to be a useful starting block from which later political and electoral reforms would emerge. The King's motive for introducing this legislation is less than clear, although it did come at a time when, as we have already remarked, there were political tensions in the country at large and particularly among the younger generation – who by this point posed a considerable demographic threat.

At the same time tensions between the Palestinian and East Bank communities had eased – much of this being down to intermarriage and an increase in prosperity of middle class Palestinians who were taking over much of the Kingdom's commercial private sector. Although Palestinians remained barred from senior jobs in the armed and security forces they had penetrated into the higher echelons of the bureaucracy. Senior members of the 'old' pre-1948 Palestinian establishment routinely filled ministerial portfolios in successive governments.

By the late 1980s Jordan's population explosion had resulted in a kingdom of which at least 50 per cent of the population were Palestinian in origin. In addition, the Palestinian Intifada or uprising of 1987 and the resurrection of the PLO as sole legitimate representatives of the Palestinian people on the world stage had sounded the death knell to Jordan's political ambitions in the West Bank and Arab East Jerusalem. While the legal status of the 1950 annexation placed West Bank territory firmly in Jordanian hands, public sympathy did not. Indeed, within the first year of the Intifada, the backlash against the Jordanian claim to the West Bank was palpable throughout the West Bank and pro-Jordanian notables were riled by a new leadership of the uprising bent on realising a nationalist dream which excluded Jordan in the equation. In this respect it should be remembered that the Intifada symbolised more than a 'shaking off' of the Israeli occupation and rejection of Israel's authority, but represented a wide-scale revolution and revolt against any claim to authority outside the newly empowered Palestinian communities of the West Bank and Gaza Strip. Some of the local activists even wanted to distance themselves from the PLO leadership in Tunis.

While the leadership in Tunis was able to re-assert its authority and harness the Intifada (albeit in competition with Islamist forces), King Hussein and his supporters were not. This prompted him to make a momentous decision regarding Jordan's relationship with the West Bank and its claims therein. On July 31 1988 the King appeared on television and in a major speech announced the unprecedented step of relinquishing all Hashemite claim to the territory of the West Bank and thereby publicly recognising the change in the status quo wrought by the Intifada and the PLO's new position. Jordan would downsize its administrative and legal commitments to the West Bank, although the issue of Hashemite custodianship of Jerusalem's Muslim Holy places including the Dome of the Rock, al-Aqsa mosque and the *Waqf* administration would remain unchanged. By this act Abdullah's grandson finally ended his grandfather's dream of expanding the Hashemite Kingdom. The King probably had no choice, as Talhami remarks, 'Without the Intifada and its real expression of hostility towards Hussein, this step would never have been possible. Its immediate outcome was the suspension of Jordan's financial obligations towards 24,000 West Bank civil employees ... There was no denying, however, that the Jordanian-PLO relationship had changed dramatically and that the umbilical cord had been severed' (Talhami, 1991, p. 234).

In terms of the domestic scene, this act of severance cemented a new era of relations with Jordan's Palestinians, characterised by newly-founded Jordanian confidence in the loyalty of its Palestinians to their East Bank refuge and a rapid rapprochement of PLO-Hashemite relations within the country. And the regime felt some relief at being relinquished from the West Bank burden, which had included a commitment to fund a bureaucratic infrastructure of considerable pro-portions (including a $40 million budget allocation for the salaries of those employed in the administration of the West Bank).

The impact of the decision to cut the territorial link with the West Bank resulted in further immediate benefits to the Kingdom. Aid programmes involving millions of dollars were scrapped, releasing resources for assisting those in the East Bank at a time when the Kingdom was experiencing major economic difficulties. The King used his prerogative to announce the dissolution of the House of Representatives, of which some 40 of the 80 elected representatives had been drawn from the West Bank. A newly constituted House of Representatives – when it eventually emerged – would now consist of members who were representatives of the Jordanian electorate rather than a mix of Jordanian and Palestinians under Israeli occupation in the West Bank. For East Bankers the impact of these decisions along with other announcements made by King Hussein in the summer of

1988 were important for at least two main reasons. Firstly: the changes were viewed as a positive step, according to Robins 'because they [East Bankers] believe that the King should stop flirting with the Palestinian cause and should divert all his energies to being the monarch of a consolidated East Bank state'. And secondly, 'because anxiety at trying to undercut the PLO ... and the enmity of which, can result only in the political and economic weakening of the Kingdom' (Robins, 1989, p. 171). In other words, the lessons of the Black September experience and its aftermath were not lost on the Jordanians.

The sentiments of many East Bankers or Transjordanians at the worsening economic situation became a major vehicle for political changes in the early months of 1989. As we will see in chapter three, by the late 1980s the Jordanian economy had hit a major crisis characterised by spiralling inflation, major foreign debt and rising unemployment. Corruption among Jordan's political elite only added to a growing sense of grievance among the urban masses, particularly in the less-prosperous southern towns and cities. By the end of 1988 and early 1989 the government was forced to implement an IMF rescue package for the ailing economy. In common with IMF conditionality elsewhere in structural adjustment programmes, the government was committed to end subsidies over a wide range of basic commodities, including staple foodstuffs such as rice and flour. Accordingly the populace at large was faced for the first time with the consequences of decades of economic mismanagement.

Genuine hardship, declining standards amongst middle-class Jordanians and widespread outrage at the levels of senior government corruption at a time when many loyal Jordanians were faced with abject poverty (30 percent of the population was below the poverty line) led to an outburst of popular indignation in the south of the country. For five days in April 1989 serious disturbances were reported in the hitherto loyalist East Banker strongholds of towns like Ma'an, Karak and Tafila. With the King absent on a visit abroad, the Crown Prince Hassan struggled to bring the situation under control. Demonstrators demanded the resignation of government ministers and called for wide-scale political reforms, including demands for 'the resignation of [Prime Minister] Rifai, a change in the electoral laws away from confessional/ethnic lines, punishment of officials for corruption, an end to austerity measures and greater democratisation' (Amawi, 1992, p. 27). Had the protest largely issued from Palestinian quarters from refugee camps on the outskirts of the capital Amman they would have evinced a different response; they, however, remained largely quiet. The protests came from the heartland of the state and reflected concern not only at the economic crisis the country faced but also reflected a conviction among many Transjordanians that they had become a disadvantaged minority in their own land. The demographic tide had finally turned on the Transjordanian population as the Palestinian community expanded in size. Transjordanians, therefore, were for their part demanding new constitutional and other guarantees for their political future.

The King responded to the spring riots with impressive alacrity and in his own inimitable style, literally going to the people and listening to their grievances. The liberalisation process, as discussed below, was the most significant outcome of these protests and while elections were the most visible signal that things were changing, the King did go some way to addressing the Transjordanian identity issue. One outcome of the pressure for political change from Transjordanians was an amendment to the electoral law, which weighted the rural constituencies at the expense of the urban ones. Such gerrymandering, according to Salibi, 'would preserve their [East Bankers] traditional majority status in parliamentary representation, on the grounds that they were the original Jordanians who had always provided the country with its backbone' (Salibi, 1993, p. 271).

THE GULF WAR: ISOLATION AND DESOLATION

The impact of the Gulf crisis following Iraq's occupation of Kuwait in August 1990 has been much remarked upon in terms of the Middle East as a whole. While much attention has been focused on players in the conflict such as Iraq, Kuwait, Saudi Arabia and the Palestinians, the effects of the crisis in Jordan were less widely acknowledged by the international community. Jordan's difficulties, for example vis-à-vis the impact of the sanctions regime against Iraq and its effects on the Jordanian economy, have been recognised to some extent though not widely publicised. The United Nations does allow the Jordanians to import oil from Iraq and associated trading provision as recognition of Jordan's special vulnerability. In addition since the early 1990s elements of European Union assistance to the country have taken account of Jordan's position. Yet, the impact on the internal dynamic of politics in the kingdom as well as foreign relations (which are examined in chapter four) was significant and resonates with as much relevance today as it did in the early 1990s.

Without a doubt, it was the popular response to Saddam Hussein's invasion of Kuwait which propelled King Hussein along a political tightrope of unseemly ambivalence, for which the entire country was to suffer international condemnation. The instinctive wave of support for Iraq as it faced up to the military might of the Desert Storm alliance was the factor which generated Jordanian refusal to join the alliance. While King Hussein condemned Iraq's attack and invasion of sovereign Kuwaiti territory, the population of his kingdom took to the streets and protested against Western interference in Arab business. The King felt he had no option but to respond to public pressure by channelling popular demands into an attempt at concocting an (obviously unrealistic) Arab solution to the crisis. He realised he had now to contend with a population, encouraged by the new era of political liberalisation and greater press freedoms, who felt able to exploit their new found confidence to push for further democratisation in the form of a positive government response to the popular will.

Behind much of this new political activity, which although ostensibly organised in the context of external developments, was the Islamic movement who perceived this as an important opportunity to consolidate their political position. When Saddam Hussein raised the banner of Islam in the 'Mother of all Battles' – justifying his assault against Kuwait as a move against Israel – he encouraged Jordan's Islamists to reiterate the same message at home. King Hussein, with an astute nose for the politics of the street, attempted a policy of co-opting the Islamists. In truth the war engendered a historic coalition of political forces, and as a result the King felt it wise to allow the Islamists considerable political freedom if only as a short term tactical device. This is seen in the appointment, following their considerable success in previous parliamentary elections, for the first time ever, of seven Islamists to Jordan's twenty-seven strong ministerial team in the short-lived cabinet of January 1991.

In parliament a broad coalition of cross-party forces emerged. Setting aside usual factional differences, they united in support of the street and the King. Unity within, however, did not inure the country to the censure of the international community nor the sanctions imposed on the country by Jordan's Gulf colleagues in the wake of the crisis. In addition, strain was put on the country's infrastructure with the arrival of 300,000 Palestinian workers who were expelled from the Gulf. Within a year the financial cost to the country was estimated to run into billions of dollars. In fact despite Jordanian disclaimers the

Gulf refugees were a blessing in one sense, bringing in savings and investing in real estate which would promote a building boom which endures to the present. This was offset, however, by the loss of regular hard currency remittances to the Jordanian economy and savings in Jordanian banks sent in by the refugees when they had been working in Kuwait and Saudi Arabia. Though the country could ill-afford the economic punishments meted out by disgruntled Gulf leaders, or the impact of UN Sanctions on its own economic links with Iraq, with time, it has recovered and has been nowhere near as damaged as at one time seemed likely. The King, in terms of short-term popular support, was the big winner. He enjoyed unprecedented heights of popularity among his citizens and his internal credibility was restored to previously undreamed of scale.

DEMOCRATISING JORDAN?

The events of spring 1989 brought home to the leadership of the country that it could no longer remain inured from the political impact of regional and local economic crisis. It is interesting to examine the particular path of change which the monarch embarked on and the pressures which propelled him along that path. A number of factors need to be identified to explain why after twenty-two years of virtual dictatorship, the King of Jordan embarked on a path of political liberalisation which would open up political life to a larger number of Jordanian citizens than ever before.

If the food riots of spring 1989 were not a serious threat to the stability of the regime, why had they promoted or prompted the King to inaugurate a period of accelerated political change in the country? One explanation can be found in the nature of these protests and the socio-economic profile of the protesters. The spring riots had, of course, been precipitated by the economic crisis, which gripped the country and had impacted on all sectors of society. Indeed, there was little the government could do to inure any of its citizens from spiralling price rises, inflation and unemployment. While in the past the spectre of real poverty may have stalked only the refugee camps, the hitherto privileged Transjordanian population was hard hit by the economic mismanagement and government corruption which had played a large part in precipitating it. In socio-economic terms this meant that contrary to patterns of protest in the past, the Spring riots started in the south of the country where those most loyal to the monarchy resided; while Palestinians also rioted they were not alone and did not reflect a purely Palestinian agenda. In other words the most loyal subjects of the King staged a revolt which clearly indicated a serious crisis of confidence at a time when the country was already beset by economic chaos.

The King's decision to institute a significant degree of political liberalisation was also influenced by three further factors affecting the stability of the prevailing political system. The first factor was external in origin and linked to pressure being exerted on the King by western and international agencies, including aid-donors such as the United States government. Western and global funding sources were applying pressure on the ruler of Jordan to pay back debt and restructure the Jordanian economy in exchange for international economic support. Grants, loans and structural adjustment assistance were increasingly linked to the political as well as economic health of the nation. There is little doubt that the democratisation/economic assistance mantra (often referred to as 'good governance') reached Hashemite ears with significant effect.

The second factor emphasises the argument put forward by Huntington who asserts that oligarchies such as those in Jordan will choose democratisation over other options as a means of regime survival, 'prolonging their own rule, achieving international legitimacy and minimising domestic opposition' (Huntington, 1984, p. 212). In other words 'defensive democracy' was very much the order of the day. The monarch had indeed, as outlined above, survived tremendous political upheavals and threats to his rule. He had responded to these threats with a variety of political strategies and tactics designed to shut out political participation in the affairs of the country. However, by 1989 the failure of other political strategies linked to economic recession may have propelled him to accept a new option. In this respect King Hussein was not unique. Rather, his strategic choices reflected the global dimension of the democracy debate. Where as Whitehead argues, 'a return to democracy no longer seemed so dangerous ... [and] all main contenders for power were therefore forced to conclude that they would do better by settling for a 'second-best' outcome' (Whitehead, 1992, p. 148). Indeed definitions of democracy and democratic intentions should be scrutinised carefully in the Jordanian context, for they reveal the paradox of an apparently democratising King who had no real intention of ever really relinquishing power to anyone outside his own family circle.

While in many respects the Palestinian issue as a threat to the state had been laid to rest by the late 1980s, the legacy of power concentrated into the hands of the few since 1957 had given rise to a tradition of autocratic rule. This was described by Samuel Finer in 1970 as a 'facade democracy': where 'historic oligarchies govern from behind a facade of liberal-democratic forms which serve as a screen for their rule' (Finer, 1970, p. 124). The palace rather than the people ruled the political roost in Jordan for many decades, making the kingdom, even in the aftermath of apparent political liberalisation, ripe for the appellation of 'monarchical democracy'. Liberalised autocracy rather than democracy prevailed and the opposition remained largely circumscribed, forced underground by the security network which hounded it. In this shackled political arena only one other political actor stood apart from the palace and those tribal leaders whose fealty lay with the King: the Islamist movement (Milton-Edwards, 1991). However, the Islamist movement, primarily the Muslim Brotherhood, acted largely as a movement of loyal opposition doing little if anything to actually threaten the status quo of Hashemite hegemony. Although the Muslim Brotherhood had not been outlawed in 1957 when all other political parties were banned there was a price to pay for survival, and the leadership of the organisation pursued a policy of abstaining from any serious opposition to the regime or its policies.

King Hussein, aware of the increased pressure from below as a result of the spring riots, for political concession of some sort announced that for the first time in twenty-two years full elections to the country's parliament would be held in November 1989. In addition a royal decree was announced abolishing special provision of seats in parliament for West Bank Palestinians and increasing the total number of seats for election to eighty. It was widely believed that the monarch had decided to embark on a process of 'democratisation' that would encourage greater plurality of opinion, increased opportunities for participation and more freedom of speech and assembly. Reforms were also said to be aimed (somewhat optimistically) at tackling the high levels of corruption, which had jeopardised the business of government. Economic crisis had severely weakened the King's coercive powers as Jordanian citizens demanded greater freedoms at a time when the IMF was making it clear that any assistance could be dependent on some liberalisation of political control.

The events since 1989 have gone some way to meeting expectations but are still treated with understandable scepticism. Jordan's path to political liberalisation is a marked improvement with regard to the extent of popular participation over the system it replaced. But it still in many ways reflects Ayubi's depiction of cosmetic democratisation as 'for the Yankees to see' and must be viewed as part of a continuing process in which the destination, a Hashemite defined genuine constitutional monarchical democracy, is still a long way off (Ayubi, 1997, p. 363).

Scepticism in certain quarters notwithstanding, the election that was held in November 1989 was regarded as a rare example of a wide measure of democracy in action in the Arab world and judged a roaring success. The campaign and polling day were the freest ever experienced in the country. Although it should be noted that political parties were still prohibited, the press remained censored and human rights abuses continued to be reported by organisations like Amnesty International (Milton-Edwards, 1996).

Nevertheless, Jordanians grasped the opportunity to participate in their political system in great numbers with an unprecedented 70 per cent of the electorate casting a vote on Election Day. The streets of the Jordanian capital, Amman, were liberally covered in election banners, and leaflets published by various political groups with candidates standing in the election were strewn throughout the major centres of population. Election fever gripped the nation while the carefully regulated press debated little else day and night. The elections to the eighty-seat House of Representatives, the lower house of the parliament, resulted in an Islamist success, delivering thirty-four seats to a variety of candidates including those aligned to the Muslim Brotherhood as well as a number of independents. The rest of the seats were distributed to leftist candidates who polled a paltry 12 seats, loyal Transjordanian tribal leaders and notables. However, the Cabinet and Senate, the upper house of parliament, still remained subject to appointment by the King himself. Some observers regarded this as unfortunate as the allegation of corruption which had so severely undermined confidence in the Hashemite monarchy had not centred on the lower house of parliament but rather on the membership of the upper which remained untouched by the reforming hand of the monarch. The King also maintained the power to dissolve parliament and to call an election whenever he chose.

From 1989 onwards, aspects of political liberalisation have been episodic in nature combined with an almost inexorable deterioration of certain freedoms once granted. Up to his final illness, King Hussein continued with plans to push for greater political and economic liberalisation of society at a pace dictated by the palace. The schedule for change has been step-by-step, with high-ranking figures such as the former Crown Prince Hassan selling this strategy as a need to recognise that 'change in the Middle East must be gradual and sensitive to the political cultural and social needs of the population. It must develop organically and not be imported wholesale; with the will to change and coming at once from above and below' (Prince Hassan bin Talal, 1992, p. 5).

Further advances were incorporated in 1992 in the National Charter, which called for greater freedom for the individual and equality in society including the establishment of a multiparty-party system and greater freedom for the press. Notably, particularly in relation to the debate about the compatibility of Islam and democracy, the Jordanian charter also enshrined the principle of Islamic law by declaring that *Shari'a* (Islamic law) would be the 'principal source of legislation' in the kingdom (Point four, Chapter 1 of the National Charter). Critics complained that such steps would only inhibit democratic mechanisms rather than encourage them, thwarting the secularist pro-democracy agenda. In the same year, the King permitted the legal formation and registration of political parties and announced that further elections to the House of Representatives would be held in 1992. Those elections resulted in a significant fall in the Islamist vote (although the Islamic Action Front remained the biggest bloc) and mainly due to the unequal weighting of constituencies, further consolidation of the traditional tribal allegiances to the King.

Since 1992 the pace of reform in the country has slowed and curbs on the press and informal political bodies like the professional associations have been reintroduced. Jordan is no police state on the Syrian or Iraqi model. But freedom of speech is not absolute, and public protest against official government policy – whether it be domestic or regional – is hazardous and when it is permitted is largely circumscribed by the presence of the security services. An indication that all was not well with the early promise of democratisation became increasingly apparent in the regime's treatment of the country's home-grown Islamic opposition, which by the mid-1990s had become a significant feature of the local political arena. Indeed the climate of political change had not improved the fortunes of the Islamist movement, its popularity and success increasingly undermined by a policy within the royal court to exaggerate its threat and undermine its credibility. By 1993 the notion that radical aspects of Islamic fundamentalism posed a very real political threat to Jordan was being highlighted through a series of arrests, show-trials, and anti-Islamist press campaigns in the country. While some Islamist groups had allowed themselves to be co-opted into the new political arena a new opposition to change emerged – led by young educated and outspoken critics of the top-down process of liberalisation, it cynically questioned the motives of the 'benevolent' king. Indeed the King's response to this challenge from within only served to highlight the fears of Islamists as opponents were rounded-up by the authorities, a number tortured, tried in military courts, refused reasonable legal representation and sentenced to death. (None, however, were executed in accordance with King Hussein's habitual policy of reluctance to create martyrs). The legacy of this encounter was reflected in a somewhat cynical response within the kingdom to further opportunities for participation in the political life of the country. That said, King Abdullah II has promised further measures of liberalisation including reform of the press laws, but the highlight of his reign by late 1999 was the exiling of the Hamas leadership which does nor augur well for continuing participation by radical Islamic groups in the Kingdom's political processes.

While the formal process of elections has been maintained with a further third general election in November 1997, popular confidence in the democratisation process has been undermined by the continuing grip on political life exerted by the monarchy. It has even been argued that by single-mindedly pursuing his peace agenda with Israel (against the general and popular will of the Jordanian people) the King himself reversed the process of liberalisation. A Jordanian commentator writing about the general elections of 1997 claimed that peace with Israel killed democracy in Jordan, because the population has been so resistant to the idea of peace and normalisation with Israel. The King, according one former high-ranking British official in Jordan, 'pulled out all the stops – constitutional and non-constitutional – to ensure normalisation. To that end pliant governments have been chosen, professional organisations muzzled, critical newspapers closed, parliament browbeaten and pressurised and parliamentary elections ... manipulated to ensure the return of members who will follow the government's policies with regard to the peace process. All this resulting in the marginalisation of parliament and popular disillusionment with the political system'.

While Jordan has gone some way in addressing its economic difficulties and re-structuring the economy, in terms of the liberalisation agenda it has been less successful. In particular there is much to be done to root out corruption, to absorb into the economy the thousands of Gulf returnees following the debacle of 1990–91 and to extract the much-vaunted peace dividend out of its treaty with Israel in 1994 (although this is mostly the fault of the previous Israeli Likud government). While a trend towards some form of liberalisation in Jordan is discernible (and may even be the most advanced within the Arab world), it was motivated by the late monarch's skill for pragmatism in responding to pressure from the middle classes for greater political freedoms and international pressure, linked with economic aid, aid which Jordan desperately needed. At the end of the 1990s all of these variables became increasingly difficult to predict, particularly the nature and form of monarchical rule in the kingdom following the demise of King Hussein.

At the beginning of the 1990s Jordan was often cited as the most encouraging example of democratisation in the region. By the middle of the decade, however, more circumspect analysis emerged calling for a proper assessment of the conditions of change that were prevailing in the country. Jordan has not democratised successfully, but then there is strong evidence to suggest that democratisation was never truly the aim of the ruling regime. Rather, appropriate conditions were created to maintain a 'façade or paper democracy', satisfying both local demands for greater participation and international and particularly American conditions at the beginning of the decade, of liberalisation for aid-giving and other financial assistance (Milton-Edwards, 1993). By the end of the 1990s the Americans were not *au fond* concerned with the active pursuit of the liberalisation agenda but with maintaining friendly regimes in the region which were compatible with US policy objectives of a sustainable (if one-sided) Arab-Israeli peace process and caging Saddam Hussein in Iraq. Any notion of US conditionality regarding democratisation and aid assistance was, therefore, not actively pursued. Their continued financial assistance despite the reversal of liberalisation and allegations of human rights abuses, depended on the assessment that the King was good for peace because of his personal relationship with Israel and the fact that Jordan presented possibilities in the campaign against Iraq. No doubt they will lean heavily on King Abdullah II to pursue the same policies, even if this means cracking down on popular discontent via unconstitutional means. In addition the process of political liberalisation in evidence at the beginning of the decade has been met with a series of reversals. This was because the Kingdom has faced further internal crisis due to factors such as peace with Israel, the continuing political fall-out of the Gulf crisis and the succession crisis prompted by King Hussein's episodes of cancer throughout the late 1990s. It is still too early to be sure if his death in February 1999 will accelerate the process of liberalisation. The possibilities are examined in our last chapter.

# Chapter 3

## THE ECONOMY

### INTRODUCTION

Jordan is a country short of natural resources – especially exploitable minerals, raw materials, water and good agricultural land. It was probably sufficient to support the 400,000 to 450,000 or so inhabitants of Transjordan at independence in 1946. But an undeveloped economy could not cope with the trebling of the population by 1950 as a result of the acquisition of the West Bank and East Jerusalem. In addition the economic infrastructure had to bear the additional responsibility of accommodating half a million Palestinian refugees who fled from their homes from inside the newly established State of Israel.

Since the 1950s economic factors have been a major issue in setting the shape of the state in Jordan. As Luciani has remarked, 'the importance of economic foundations of state structures' cannot be underestimated when examining the shape of 'the basic parameters of Arab politics' (Luciani, 1990, p. 65). From these foundations Jordan emerges as a certain economic type within the region. Economists such as Luciani would be inclined to remark on the country's relationship in terms of the allocation and production states of the region being inextricably linked to the development of the Middle East in terms of hydrocarbon resources. In this context Jordan could not be described as a 'rentier economy' in the purest sense of directly living off the rents earned from oil production and the ripple effects this has on other aspects of the economy. Unlike Kuwait or Saudi Arabia it has no oil worth mentioning. Jordan has been recognised as having an economy that was excessively dependent on 'workers remittances becoming one of the major foreign exchange sources' leaving the national economy extremely vulnerable to external political and economic fluctuations (Belawi, 1990, p. 97). Given that the 350,000 or so workers were employed in oil rich states in the Gulf, this lends an indirect rentier aspect to the Jordanian economy as value of remittances at times surpassed that of exports.

At first glance this model appears to help us understand Jordan's economy and subsequent developments from the 1970s onwards. As we shall see later in this chapter, however, there are problems associated with this approach. We also need to look at the progress towards liberalisation of the economy in Jordan, given the commensurate link to the issues of external debt, foreign assistance, and the politics of economic restructuring which have preoccupied the country for more than a decade.

From its creation Jordan has relied on foreign assistance. As Issawi notes, the country has been 'heavily dependent on foreign aid, first from the United Kingdom, then from the United States and in recent years from Arab countries' (Issawi, 1982, p. 74). From the first foundations of the state, as described in the Chapter One, a British subsidy never less than £2 million a year underpinned the state's finances. Throughout Emir – later King – Abdullah's reign the economy of the state was reliant on the British subsidy, which as described in the first chapter gave considerable leverage for the protecting power. As Kingston notes, 'preoccupied with questions of order and survival, the political elites of Jordan by and large neglected the importance of promoting a programme of economic modernisation. They left that task ... to their British patrons ... and to the then newly-created US assistance programme called Point Four' (Kingston, 1994, p. 188). British control over the finance portfolio in the colonial period allowed London to dictate the manner in which the state's meagre economic resources would be distributed and in whose coffers their contribution or subsidy would land. Although the British subsidy was by no means generous it created a relationship of dependency which would characterise the economy for generations.

As the kingdom developed under King Hussein and its economy expanded so did its need for extensive external aid. The US took over the baton from Britain in the 1960s followed by the Arab oil producers in the 1970s and 80s. Since the Gulf crisis and the rupture in Arab mainly Gulf aid to Jordan the Washington based International Financial Institutions (IFIs), supported by mainly western donors, have plugged the gaps. The death of King Hussein in February 1999, however, has allowed his successor to seek an all-important diplomatic as well as economic rapprochement with the Gulf aid-givers.

The Kingdom has always needed this aid to survive but resented the necessity of having to live off it. As one writer observed: 'The history of Hashemite Jordan is as much coloured by a continual struggle against dependence on outside financial support as it is by an uphill battle for political recognition and legitimacy' (Satloff, 1994, p. 5).

Much of this struggle seemed hopeless and occurred against the background of almost cataclysmic events: the 1967 'Six Day War' which caused the loss of the West Bank and the doubling of the refugee problem, the civil war of 1970–1 between the Palestine Liberation Army (PLO) and the Hashemite army in support of the monarchy and, most recently, the Kuwait crisis of 1990–91. This created more refugees, this time from the Gulf, and meant both the loss of their remittances and the long-term loss of much of the lucrative Iraq market because of UN sanctions.

Economic self-sufficiency and directing the development of the economy to this end remains a government priority and is one of the long-term objectives of the current IMF/IBRD supported structural adjustment programme. This is unlikely to be achieved in the absence of a comprehensive and lasting solution to the Arab-Israeli dispute and the full return of Iraq to the international community following the lifting of sanctions. Even in favourable circumstances, the Jordanian economy will still have a long way to go before it can operate confidently on the basis of its own resources. In particular it will have to alleviate its crippling debt burden accumulated over a generation of good times and bad. Recent figures distributed by the Jordanian government put the debt at US\$ 6.8 billion and the annual debt servicing requirement at US\$ 800 million (Marto, 1999, p. 1).

## THE DEVELOPMENT OF THE MODERN ECONOMY 1948–1980

By the late 1940s the essential ingredients of Jordanian economic life had been established. The economy could be characterised as agricultural and peasant-based – much of the population were engaged in farming or were nomads or semi-nomads raising livestock. Traditional farming practices prevailed in a largely arid region, with sparse and erratic rainfall. Indeed water and its shortages was a natural enemy of the development of Jordan's agricultural sector. Nevertheless, by the 1950s agricultural production in the country had increased and developed although this was still rarely more than a subsistence economy east of the Jordan. Land-ownership, according to Issawi, was predominantly in the form of small-holdings, which by the 1950s resulted in '53 per cent of private land in holdings of 20 hectares or less, 33 in holdings of 20–100 hectares and 14 per cent in holdings of 100 hectares' (Issawi, 1982, p. 149). Transjordan was much less developed than its neighbour Palestine to the west. There was little industry apart from some handicrafts and foreign tourists were virtually unknown. The development of Petra and the other historic sites had not begun – commercial tourism was virtually confined to old Jerusalem and Bethlehem on the West Bank. Jordan's port, Aqaba, remained undeveloped at a time when Suez and Haifa on the Mediterranean coast provided all the access and trade routes the British needed. Despite this the country did still benefit from some passing pilgrim trade as many Muslims crossed the country on hajj to Saudi Arabia. In this respect the Hijaz railway served a useful income generating purpose.

The first Arab-Israeli war of 1948 and the subsequent incorporation of a large part of the West Bank (5,600 sq. km.) into the Hashemite Kingdom made a major impact on the economy. A large and productive agricultural area together with East (or 'Arab') Jerusalem became integral parts of the Jordan economy, remaining so until the loss of the West Bank as a result of the 1967 war. In 1948–9 the population of the country trebled, including Palestinians fleeing from the territory of the newly established State of Israel. When Israel occupied the West Bank, salient after its comprehensive victory in 1967, about 350,000 of its Palestinian inhabitants fled to East Bank Jordan, once again restricted to its pre-1948 *de jure* borders.

The 1979 Census gave the population as 2.1 million – an annual growth rate of 4.8 per cent – of which immigration accounted for 1 per cent. This rapid population expansion would later be exacerbated by a natural population boom in the country with an accelerated growth rate of 2.6 per cent per year between 1965–1980 and 3.7 per cent in the period 1980–85 (Richards and Waterbury, 1990, p. 83). Despite government attempts and campaigns to slow the population growth rate, a decade later the figures for annual growth had reached an alarming 5.7 per cent per year, considerably higher than most other countries in the region. This rapid increase in the population made it necessary to import large amounts of food and other commodities and a massive expansion of the transport infrastructure to move the goods. Indeed, despite developments in the agricultural sector such as a move to mechanisation and a decline in agricultural labour Jordan became increasingly dependent on food imports; the proportion was 19 per cent of the total to the country in 1985 (World Bank, 1987, p. 231). Paying for imports has not been balanced by, for example, a healthy profit on export of manufactured goods and has, therefore, increased Jordan's indebtedness abroad. All of this has turned food security into a major political issue in Jordan and presented the government with considerable headaches in terms of economic planning, economic adjustment programmes and breaking the debt and dependency.

Since 1948 Jordan had been denied access to the (now Israeli controlled) Mediterranean ports and a start was made on a crash programme for developing Aqaba, the port town to the south of the country neighbouring Saudi Arabia. A comprehensive road network was established and generally government services including health and education had to expand to meet the changed circumstances. Perforce, the economy rapidly switched from one where agriculture was the primary activity to a services dominated one. By 1978 agriculture contributed JD 51 million to a total GDP of JD 471 million whilst government services including transport and communications accounted for JD 165 million. When other services such as financial are included, the services sector contributed 63 per cent of GDP, almost double the 37 per cent from industry, agriculture and construction combined (Nyrop, 1980, p. 108).

Despite the preponderance of the services sector, there was considerable expansion in industry, construction, trade and banking – admittedly from a very low base – and new modern industries such as phosphate, cement and oil refining (Jordan imported all its crude oil requirements as it still does). Smaller manufacturing industries sprang up. Irrigation enabled agricultural output to expand by about 7 per cent a year. A construction boom catered for the demand for housing and for the expansion of the road and rail network. Tourism also became an important source of revenue – particularly Jordanian controlled East Jerusalem, which included the sites of the Church of the Holy Sepulchre and al-Aqsa mosque in the Old City.

The first surge of growth was from 1953 until 1967 – surprisingly so, given Jordan's natural geophysical disadvantages. Pundits had been pessimistic about Jordan's economic prospects at the start of King Hussein's reign. With minimal resources and little land not already under cultivation, the problem of creating employment for a suddenly increased population was daunting. Nevertheless despite most unpromising circumstances economic growth up to the 1967 war was astonishingly high. Between 1954 and 1967 prices remained stable and GNP increased at more than 8 per cent a year in real terms (11 per cent at current prices), one of the highest growth rates in the world at that time (Nyrop, 1980, p. 108). Although Jordan was highly dependent on foreign aid it was the efficient management of this assistance which was mainly responsible for this remarkable performance.

A serious interruption to the record of sustained growth was the 1967 war, which has already briefly been alluded to. In addition to the sudden increase in the flow of refugees, Jordan lost over a third of its best agricultural land and most of its foreign exchange earnings from tourism (a trickle of tourists to Jerash and Petra were poor compensation for the loss of Bethlehem and Jerusalem). The damage to GDP may have been as high as 40 per cent. With the Suez Canal still closed until mid 1975, most imports and exports were re-routed via Lebanese and Syrian ports thus adding significantly to trading costs and affecting the flow of trade. All this was exacerbated by the disruption caused by Israeli retaliatory raids against Palestinian guerrilla bases (thus making parts of the fertile Jordan Valley untenable by farmers). The Jordanian-Palestinian civil war of 1970–1 caused further problems. The Syrian border was closed for 18 months and various Arab countries halted their aid to Jordan to protest against the measures taken against the Palestinian leadership. Jordan's expenditure on arms substantially increased in this period replacing equipment destroyed in 1967 and reflecting a new phase of confrontation against Israel as enshrined in the Khartoum Declaration.

This episode of what Feiler described as under development proved to be short-lived and after the 1973 Arab-Israeli war (which Jordan prudently sat out) the growth rate actually accelerated – in current prices-to a phenomenal 20 per cent per year (Feiler, 1994, p. 45). All sectors of the economy contributed, especially mining and manufacturing. The period up to the end of the decade witnessed a substantial increase in output and prices for phosphates. A booming domestic market benefited manufacturing, as did expanding demand in the Arabian Peninsular fed by rapidly increasing oil prices. This sector rose by 29 per cent a year and agriculture by 24 per cent. Although these GDP figures need to be treated with some caution and should be put into the context of rapidly spiralling prices, economists such as Day agree that real growth was substantial at about 8 per cent – amongst the highest in the world (Day, 1998, p. 648). By 1980 Jordan was classified as a medium-sized lower-middle income country. But economic growth still in part depended on substantial foreign aid inflows, including significant Arab financial support which had been restored after 1972. Foreign aid income accounted for between at least 25 per cent and sometimes over 60 per cent of import earnings between 1972 and 1980 (Seccombe and Wilson, 1987, p. 6).

Concern over foreign aid dependency not withstanding, the resumption of rapid economic growth had beneficial political side effects. Much of the kingdom's new found stability post-1973 was due to the economy's ability to satisfy the needs and aspirations of a substantial proportion of the population, even if incomes varied markedly between the more affluent urban areas and poorer rural dwellers. In this respect Jordan's economy was developing all the least desirable attributes of a modern Arab state, including problems of urbanisation and excessive energy uses, a weak agricultural sector and aid dependent development. The late 1970s saw the first serious efforts by the government to include social welfare measures as an integral part of economic planning. But the boom provided opportunities for individual enterprise and upward mobility for a workforce benefiting from the expansion in secondary and higher education. The frenetically growing demand for skilled workers in the Gulf attracted thousands of Jordanians (mostly Palestinian-Jordanians) to the benefit of Jordan through the receipt of remittances by families or savings accounts in commercial banks. These were worth JD 236 million ($700m) in 1980 not much below the level of foreign aid inflows for that year and double the value of the country's exports (Seccombe and Wilson, 1987, p. 6).

Palestinians domiciled in Jordan were not only going to the Gulf but were also increasingly involved in domestic commercial activity and being steadily and profitably absorbed into the economy. Because of lingering doubts about their loyalty in the wake of Black September they found it hard to aspire to senior posts in government and were largely shut out of the defence and security establishment. Nevertheless this group became a new class in its own right – one which had gained a stake in the Jordanian state through success in the private sector. This economic activity started a trend, still prevalent today, with most non-governmental economic and commercial activity in the country increasingly controlled by a Palestinian middle class, thus ensuring a high degree of involvement in and commitment to their new home. The most significant political spin-off was growing support by the Palestinian-Jordanian middle class for the Hashemite regime. This amounted to a recognition by many middle income Palestinians that Jordan as a legitimate entity, separate from any future Palestinian state, could provide a homeland for a substantial number of Palestinians whose primary economic loyalty lay with the Hashemites.

Despite the continued regional instability caused by the Arab-Israeli confrontation and the outbreak of a major war in the Gulf between Iraq and Iran, the period of rapid and sustained growth continued until 1981. Jordan's political and commercial tilt towards Iraq brought the economy some immediate benefits. With Iraq's Gulf ports threatened by the Iranian navy, Aqaba, in southern Jordan, became Iraq's principal maritime outlet – Jordan prospering from the transit trade. In 1982, of the 30,000 containers transiting the port, 18,000 were to or from Iraq (Seccombe and Wilson, 1987, p. 21). In 1980 and 1981 the two countries signed a series of trade and aid agreements, cementing the economic relationship. In 1981 Jordan's exports to Iraq were $187m compared with $43m in 1979 making Iraq by far its largest market. Apart from some blips caused by the Iran-Iraq Gulf war, exports remained at a high level throughout the decade. They were partially underpinned by an oil-for-goods barter arrangement foreshadowing Jordan's current (but much reduced) economic relationship with Iraq. Indeed Jordan's over dependence on Iraq as its principal market dates from this time and this is still a major factor in exacerbating present economic difficulties. A high proportion of Jordanian goods was made especially for the Iraqi market. Thus a market circumscribed by UN sanctions since 1990 has had a serious effect on a number of Jordanian companies used only to exporting to Iraq.

The years 1980 and 1981 saw record real GDP increases of 17.6 per cent and 9.8 per cent. Then came a sharp deceleration in growth: 5.6 per cent in 1982, 2.5 per cent in 1983 and 0.8 per cent in 1983. 1981 was probably the last year of a healthy economy. Some of the extraneous factors from which Jordan had benefited in the high growth seventies – particularly a 'favourable regional environment' were now absent with a full-scale war in the northern Gulf (Feiler, 1994, p. 50). Oil prices had flattened and dipped in real terms and economic activity in the wealthy Gulf States who depended on high oil prices slowed down. This hit markets important to Jordan (including Iraq itself) and seriously affected the level of remittances to Jordan from its expatriates working in the Gulf Peninsular oil states (representing 85 per cent of Jordanian expatriate workers – 340,000 in all in 1983). These declined from JD 475m in 1984 to JD317m in 1987 ($1.228m to $953m).

Given Jordan's continued dependence on aid inflows – 55 per cent of import expenditure in 1980 – it was disappointed by the failure of parties to uphold the pledge made at the 1978 Baghdad Arab Summit (Seccombe and Wilson, 1987, p. 6). Seven Arab states had promised $1250m special development aid to the Hashemite Kingdom at a meeting convened to condemn the Camp David accords between Israel and Egypt. In the event rhetoric was only translated into full commitment by Saudi Arabia. Some of the others – especially Kuwait – were supportive but not on the scale envisaged at Baghdad. After all, these states were also starting to experience a decline in economic fortunes and this affected their aid-giving capacity. In consequence, Jordan, having recorded its first current account deficit in 1981, continued to show shortfalls until 1985. The country's economy also failed to meet the targets of the 1981–85 Development Plan, which had been predicated on a level of international support which was not forthcoming.

These shortfalls were compounded by Jordan's customary trade deficit (over $2000m a year throughout the decade) made worse by the decline in the world price of Jordan's two principal exports of phosphate and potash. The manufacturing sector failed to expand despite greater diversification. Agricultural output was also flat with a continued population drift from rural areas to the towns (or abroad). Ironically although Jordan exported a high proportion of her labour force, the flight from the land obliged her to import 100,000 foreign workers by 1981, mostly from other Arab countries (Owen and Pamuk, 1998, p. 190). In response to this stagnation the government sought extra financing in the form of development loans. In the short term these additional funds led to a partial recovery in GDP growth (2.7 per cent in 1985 – trebling the growth of the previous year) but in the medium and long term added significantly to the country's foreign debt and the burden of annual repayments. By 1989 the cost of servicing this debt of $6,500m was $900m of which $500m represented annual interest. The same year inflation had risen to 25 per cent on the back of national budget deficits of 7 per cent and 6 per cent of GDP in 1987 and 1988 respectively. By November 1988 the value of the Jordanian Dinar had declined by 30 per cent during the past month and foreign currency reserves were dangerously low despite stringent new regulations.

With the economy in deep trouble the government felt obliged to intro-duce austerity measures. Bans were imposed on the import of a range of luxury items and customs duties raised on non-essential goods. Some taxes were increased and to curtail currency speculation all licences for moneychangers were cancelled. In early 1989 with some reluctance the government started negotiations with the IMF, believing that an agree-ment with the Fund was the only way it could maintain its foreign exchange reserves and finance the budget deficit (Day, 1998, p. 659). By July 1989 agreement was reached with the IMF on a stand-by credit of $125m, conditional upon the implementation of a five-year structural adjustment programme, drafted in consultation with the Fund. This had the aim, through reducing government expenditure, increasing revenues and reducing imports, of cutting the rate of inflation from 14 per cent to 7 per cent, bringing the budget deficit down to 5 per cent of GDP (24 per cent in 1988) and achieving a current account surplus and in Pfeifer's words 'a standard set of measures aimed at "getting the prices right" ' (Pfeifer, 1999, p. 23).

Standard IMF 'medicine' has almost invariably as one of its ingre-dients the reduction and eventually abolition of government subsidies on all commodities. In Jordan's case subsidies were cut on a range of goods including fuel. In addition, in April 1989 increases in taxation were announced. As described in Chapter 2 these additional hardships proved too much for a significant proportion of usually loyal citizens. They felt squeezed by the steady erosion of their living standards in a contracting economy. They were also angry at reports of large scale corruption in the higher echelons of government and the urban elite of Amman – living in the smart suburban 'Sleeping Beauty Castles' (as one Palestinian journalist described them) – who appeared to prosper as the middle class and the poor suffered. Serious and widespread disturbances erupted with the consequential change of government and other political developments described elsewhere.

## THE TURBULENT 1990s: STRUCTURAL ADJUSTMENT AND THE GULF CRISIS

The new government formed in summer 1989 led by Sherif Zeid bin Shaker committed itself to implementing the programme of structural adjustment agreed with the IMF. Such programmes, according to Pfeifer, were designed to forward 'a modern-day mission in support of world trade, finance and investment. The mission aims to convert the benighted heathen in developing countries to the enlightened religion of the free market, whose invisible hand guides self-interest toward the best possible outcome' (Pfeifer, 1999, p. 23). For Jordan this meant that the entire country would have to undergo considerable transformation to achieve the end goal. As part of this process the majority of the population would undergo extreme financial hardship while a small and privileged elite would remain corrupt and benefit disproportionately from economic recovery.

The efforts of the government started under inauspicious circumstances with a further devaluation of the Dinar – now down 42 per cent against the US Dollar in seven months. One third of the gold reserves had been exchanged for foreign exchange in 1988 and foreign debt had reached a new peak of $8,100m (Day, 1998, p. 659). Then the measures undertaken by the new administration started to have effect. The Dinar stabilised, having been pegged to a basket of currencies in which the US Dollar predominated. There was a welcome resumption of aid from Arab countries, and the 'London Club' of commercial bank creditors agreed to reschedule over half a billion US Dollars' worth of Jordan's debt. The 'Paris Club' creditor countries followed suit with official debt (debt due for repayment in 1989 and 1990 to be rescheduled over 10 years). As a result of these developments Jordan's current account moved into surplus, but inflation increased to 25 per cent, the budget remained in deficit and the country in recession. However, the slide had been halted and the basis for economic recovery – albeit at a slower rate than envisaged by the IMF – was now in place.

By mid-1990 domestic and international confidence was being restored in the economy and the government, against the background of political reform, could once again contemplate cuts in state subsidies on basic commodities (including food) without the fear of public disorder. In some respects there was cause for celebration, and the IMF's own study of the structural adjustment programme in Jordan concluded that significant progress had been achieved (Maciejewski, E. and Mansur, A, 1996). National debt and public spending deficits in Jordan have, however, economically enslaved them to the dictates of foreign government aid programmes such as those from America (which rose from $7 million in 1996 to $140 million in 1998). In addition, planning and economic policy were heavily dependent on international lending organisations like the International Monetary Fund (IMF) and World Bank. Their programmes currently include 'US$ 120 million for export development, trade liberalisation, financial sector reform, privatisation and regulatory reform,' and also 'US$60 million for Human Resources Development Sector investment' to build schools and provide equipment for them (IRBD, 1999, p. 6).

The impact of such relationships is widespread, as Ehteshami and Murphy note: 'While there may be popular consensus over the need for reform, there is decreasingly so over the strategy of economic liberalisation, and particularly IMF-negotiated structural adjustment programmes, the benefits of which are usually "deferred, uncertain and diffused"' (Ehteshami and Murphy, 1996, p. 766). Nevertheless, the virtually obligatory agenda of economic liberalisation, relinquishing state control over the economy, privatisation, foreign investment and capital and diversification of industry has resulted in only limited economic improvement in the lives of the majority of the population. The political consequences of even such faltering and minor improvements in the national economy of Jordan have been serious and characterised by an increasing tendency to reassert state authority through coercion. Ultimately economic liberalisation in Jordan, like other countries in the Third World, has neither ushered in nor encouraged democracy. Rather, as Ehteshami and Murphy argue, 'political liberalism is in retreat ... economic liberalisation creates a restructuring of interests which only consolidate and benefit the power-holders rather than the powerless, (Ehteshami and Murphy, 1996, p. 768).

### THE GULF CRISIS

Jordan's controversial reaction to Iraq's invasion of Kuwait in August 1990 and the reasons for its stance are described in Chapter Four. The political fallout from the Kingdom's self imposed isolation lingers today; the economic effects were as significant although not amounting to some of the 'worst-case' scenarios predicted at that time and since by a number of observers (Day, 1998, p. 649). The loss of all-important trade with Iraq was the first casualty of the crisis. The flow of oil from Iraq (the supplier of 80 per cent of Jordan's requirements before the war) was initially maintained by road tanker until the actual hostilities in early 1991 when alternative and expensive suppliers had to be found and rationing imposed. An immediate burden on the country's faltering and recovering economy was the upkeep and processing of a flood of new refugees – 470, 000 fled to Jordan from Kuwait in August and September 1990. At the same time tourists vanished from the region — Jordan alone losing an estimated $403m of income from tourism in 1990–91.

Remittances from expatriate workers in the Gulf worth $1.3 billion in 1989 were drastically curtailed and in the case of those in Kuwait (80 per cent of the overseas workforce) stopped completely. A Jordanian economist, Fahd al Fanek of the Jordanian Economic Monitor, calculated the immediate impact on the country's GDP to have been a further drop of 18.2 per cent (Abu-Jabarah, 1993, p. 193). But the worst and longer-term economic effects of this particular regional conflict were to make themselves felt in the immediate post-war period.

Kuwait was liberated in February 1991 and the immediate military and political crisis was over. The UN imposed comprehensive sanctions on Iraq before, during and after the hostilities. Their impact on Jordan is discussed below. Jordan's perceived ambivalence to Saddam Hussein's aggression lost it friends in the Gulf – particularly Saudi Arabia and Kuwait. The supply of cheap oil from Saudi Arabia, some 20 per cent of Jordan's fuel imports, was stopped on Saudi orders as a punitive measure designed to make King Hussein pay for his neutrality. The Saudi Arabian market representing 9 per cent of Jordan's exports was closed and transit trade of fruit and vegetables to other Gulf States blocked. Many of the 300,000 or so Jordanian-Palestinians resident in Kuwait fled during the crisis. Most of the rest who stayed were accused of sympathy for or active collaboration with the occupying Iraqis and were expelled, or if abroad were not permitted to return. Some were imprisoned in Kuwait and not released for several years. Most of those resident in Saudi Arabia were similarly repatriated and not allowed to return.

Thus Jordan lost an important source of foreign exchange previously provided through remittances and had to absorb 350,000 'returnees' as they came to be known. But their arrival was not the unmitigated disaster some Jordanian officials have claimed. Certainly the loss of a regular and substantial inflow of hard currency hit a hard-pressed economy. Moreover the sudden influx of the returnees, however highly skilled many of them were, raised the level of unemployment to 30 per cent. It is also worth noting that 80 per cent of the returnees were still unemployed after a year and put a severe strain on domestic resources and facilities – especially the housing market.

But there was also a beneficial aspect. Many of the former Gulf residents were wealthy and brought fresh capital into the Kingdom. They helped to boost construction activity by 220 per cent of its 1990 level by 1992 (Day, 1998, p. 649). Most of the spectacularly striking houses which are one of the features of modern Amman and its wealthier suburbs date from this time of frenetic construction boom. Expatriates in Kuwait not being allowed to own property was a deprivation many Jordanian-Palestinians more than made up for on their return to Jordan. The building boom, while a benefit to one sector of the economy, has had short-term effects and on the negative side has succeeded in pushing land prices sky high, increased rapid urbanisation in Amman and affected the infrastructure. Much of this 'returnee' wealth would have been of greater benefit to the local economy had it been invested in the development of the private sector, and particularly in local manufacturing industry. But only a small percentage was put aside to 'kick start' small-scale enterprises, and that not until the mid-nineties.

Various calculations have been made on the damage to the Jordanian economy by the Gulf crisis and the imposition of UN sanctions on Iraq. One forecast made by the Jordanian Ministry of Finance in October 1990 predicted a crisis-related loss of $2.14 billion. This covered loss of exports, remittances, Iraqi transit trade, tourism, increased import bills emergency relief for evacuees (Day, 1998, p. 649). A more inflated figure of over $8 billion (i.e. equivalent to twice Jordan's GDP) was produced in 1991 to include the loss of assets owned by Jordanians in Kuwait and higher oil import costs. Special pleading with one eye cocked to the international donor community was certainly a factor, and the real figure is probably considerably lower than the Jordanian estimates, but it is bad enough. IMF assessments revealed a fall in GDP of 7.9 per cent as a direct result of the crisis and its aftermath and GNP falling 17 per cent in Dollar terms. A UNICEF survey in 1991 claimed that over 30 per cent of the population were living below the official poverty line (a family income of less than $130 a month) compared to 20 per cent before the Iraqi invasion (Abu-Jabarah, 1993, p. 192). But this may have had as much to do with a long-term trend resulting from economic stagnation in the late 1980's rather than a direct consequence of the events of 1990–91. Nevertheless, there can be no doubt that the events of 1990–91 exacerbated the country's economic crisis. For example, it was during this period that per capita income fell from a peak of $2,180 in 1986 to $843 in 1990 – an annual decline of 15.25 per cent (Abu-Jabarah, 1993, p. 193).

In addition to the factors predicted by the Jordanian Ministry of Finance at the start of the crisis was the post-war refusal by Saudi Arabia and Kuwait to continue financial support for the Kingdom. The US also suspended financial aid ($60m) as a mark of disapproval at Jordan's lack of support for the Desert Storm alliance. This was perhaps more of a psychological blow than an economic one. As explained in Chapter Four it was his anxiety to mend fences with Washington which was a major influence on King Hussein's sub-sequent intense involvement in the Middle East Peace Process (MEPP), culminating in his treaty with Israel in 1994. In addition, the economic dividends of peace as extended to the Kingdom from external donors such as the US heavily influenced the King when pondering his options.

Despite initial disapproval of the Kingdom's position with regard to the Gulf crisis by most of Jordan's traditional allies in the region and in the developed world, there was soon a recognition that the country was suffering severe economic penalties through circum-stances beyond its control. Jordan had formally accepted the raft of Security Council Resolutions implementing the most comprehensive sanctions regime ever imposed on a member state by the UN. Only food, medicine and other 'humanitarian' supplies could be sent to Iraq. Its exports were banned and its overseas assets, where trace-able, frozen. The regime was isolated as an international pariah until such time as the UN was satisfied that Baghdad had implemented all its resolutions, especially in regard to the destruction of all weapons of mass destruction.

The effect on Jordan was inevitably, if incidentally, punitive. Iraq, as we have already noted, had been its biggest market, taking 23 per cent of its exports and supplying 80 per cent of its oil requirements at well below world market prices, partly because of an oil for goods barter component. Iraqi transit trade to its only accessible port had kept Aqaba at full operating capacity and transit dues (and transport profits) had made a major contribution to the Jordanian exchequer. A US led multinational naval force blockaded Aqaba, ensuring that illegal goods for Iraq were turned back. By 1994 the transit trade had declined to such an extent that the port was only operating at 50 per cent capacity.

There was a consequential effect on domestic industrial pro-ductivity. As mentioned before many small to medium sized enterprises were locked into the Iraqi market. Whole ranges of poor quality goods accepted as barter were not saleable elsewhere. The economies of scale also applied. The domestic market of fewer than four million people is a small one. Larger companies, especially in the pharmaceutical sector, lost over 70 per cent of their sales with the closure of the Iraqi market as a result of the sanctions and the Saudi and Kuwaiti one as a result of diplomatic breakdown and mutual hostility. The Ministry of Finance estimated the loss of the Iraqi and Kuwaiti markets in 1990–91 at $280m plus $169m in reduced transit fees. Many small to medium size companies went under at this time and never resumed trading.

Thanks to clever and aggressive diplomacy by the Jordanian government supported by the IMF and World Bank, much of the international community had been mobilised to come to Jordan's assistance by late 1991. King Hussein's positive and active approach to yet another US led initiative to kick start the MEPP at Madrid (see Chapter Four) 'rehabilitated' his country in Western eyes as a key player in the search for a comprehensive peace. The UN recognised the Kingdom's particular difficulties with regard to the Iraqi sanctions regime and accordingly informally endorsed an oil protocol with Baghdad. Under its provisions Jordan was able to import a combination of cheap and free oil in exchange for reducing Iraq's debt to the Kingdom. Within this agreement there were provisions for a resumption of Jordanian exports up to a prescribed annual value, but only (officially) in goods not subject to sanctions. Although undoubtedly covert, sanctions busting mostly dummy Jordanian companies fronting for Iraqi concerns took place and continues to do so. However trade with Iraq has nowhere near approached pre-crisis volumes.

As early as March 1991, pledges of special aid to Jordan channelled through the Gulf Financial Crisis Co-ordination Group (GFCCG) amounted to $1.23 billion, including a resumption of US aid. Further rescheduling of foreign debt, an IMF standby facility and this substantial external assistance enabled Jordan to weather the immediate crisis. In 1991 domestic revenue exceeded expenditure for the first time and 1992 witnessed an unexpectedly strong recovery in the economy generally. GDP shot up to 10.1 per cent as against barely 1 per cent in 1991. By 1993, with reduction of trade links with Iraq, Saudi Arabia and Kuwait not as serious as the first dire predictions had led people to believe, optimism returned. For example, new markets for the pharmaceutical industry had been found in North Africa. More debt rescheduling and with a fresh tranche of IMF assistance in support of a new programme of structural reform covering the period up to 1998, the country seemed set to meet its economic targets. Although very serious problems remained (the external debt burden was 140 per cent of GDP – 200 per cent in the 1980s – and unemployment stood at

25 per cent, with growing disparity between rich and poor, it at last seemed that the effects of the Gulf crisis had been overcome and a new period of growth embarked upon.

## THE PEACE DIVIDEND

For a country so dependent on external assistance and regional stability, economic factors inevitably have a powerful influence on foreign policy. By the same token, some of the worst economic crises in the Kingdom's history have been provoked by the triumph of political expediency (or necessity) over economic prudence. Involvement in the 1967 war and active neutrality during the Gulf crisis are cases in point. As shown in Chapter Two, King Hussein felt that he could hardly have stayed out in 1967 given the forces of rampant Arab nationalism and their effect on the Kingdom's stability. In 1990 the King purported to believe that he could not afford to ignore popular support for Iraq and join the Desert Storm Alliance. In contrast, he was largely to ignore domestic public opinion by his positive engagement in the MEPP – especially when he became only the second Arab head of state to sign a comprehensive peace treaty with Israel, the old enemy, and the first one to work for warm normalisation of relations between his country and Israel. The Egyptian-Israeli relationship established at Camp David in 1979 had rarely progressed beyond cool political correctness at a government to government level.

The political considerations are discussed in more detail elsewhere. Central to them was King Hussein's perception that Jordan, after its self-imposed isolation during the Gulf crisis, needed to resume its traditional place within an alliance of conservative Arab regimes and their western supporters. For all his high profile hankering for an Arab solution to the problem (in the circumstances oxymoronic), he had been badly shaken by the angry Western response to his refusal to confront Saddam. Economic factors also weighed heavily in his thinking, a combination of accurate calculation and, as it proved, wishful thinking especially with regard to the benefits that peace with Israel would bring to Jordan.

Yet while many purported to believe that the benefits of peace with Israel would include a significant economic dividend, the reality was that the international community – through bi-lateral and multi-lateral assistance, loans and direct aid – would shore up the economy and thus assist the regime to withstand popular discontent at the King's political gamble. The King was well aware that as part of the US strategy of trying to make a success of the Madrid negotiations, the Americans had dangled the prospect of new economic support for the main players in the event of the Middle East Peace Process showing tangible progress. Jordan was a major target for such blandishments once the PLO and Israel had signed up to the Oslo agreement in September 1993. In addition, it was argued that 'One of the primary attractions for Jordan of a regional peace deal is the opportunity it should yield for economic expansion. The kingdom is the natural commercial partner for the developing Palestinian entity and Jordanian industry has been anticipating a big jump in exports to the West Bank and Gaza Strip once Palestinian nation-building gets under way' (Edge, S. and Doughty, P., 1993, p. 2). It was clear that not only would Washington be generous with increased bilateral assistance, including the cancellation of all official and most commercial debt, but would also encourage the rest of the donor community including the Washington based International Financial Institutions (IFIs) to do likewise.

And so it proved, although debt forgiveness in the round did not turn out to be as generous as Jordan had hoped. In July 1994 Jordan and Israel agreed on the main parameters of a comprehensive peace treaty. The World Bank immediately advocated substantial foreign debt relief – a plea that fell on receptive ears in a number of donor countries. The US honoured its commitments by writing off $700m worth of debt plus commitments of $500m financial assistance over 5 years. The British converted $92m loans into grants as a signal of support for Jordan's peace policies. The British also rescheduled over $300m worth of 'Paris Club' debt, as did other creditor countries – some of whom (e.g. Germany) also entered into debt-equity swap arrangements. The rescheduling was on the back of an agreement with the IMF in May 1994 for a three year extended fund facility (worth SDR 127.8m) in support of the next phase of the structural adjust-ment programme. 'London Club' creditors had also rescheduled over $900m of commercial debt in late 1993.

Despite all this evidence of international support linked to the peace process, Jordan was disappointed that debt write-off fell well short of the $3.3 billion it had been looking for. Its biggest individual creditor, Japan (owed $1.8 billion), refused debt forgiveness as a matter of principle but provided a generous balance of payments (BOP), loan support and some debt rescheduling. The European Union also provided development funds linked to political progress within the MEPP (including $125m BOP grant support in 1996), but with the highest concentration of aid going to the emerging Palestine National Authority (PNA). According to the World Bank, Jordan benefited during this period from more donor support than any other country of its size and income level on a per capita basis. (World Bank Group Survey of Jordan, World Bank Web Site, March 1999).

Arab aid is a very important but understudied aspect of financial support to the Jordanian economy. Not only was it significant in the oil-boom years of the 1970s and early 1980s, it made an important contribution to the recovery of the Jordanian economy in the late 1990s. Although such aid declined as a result of political differences within the Arab world the Arab Fund for Economic and Social Development was the main multilateral donor to the country in 1998, supplying more than US$200 million in loan support, accounting for 53 per cent of multi-lateral aid. The majority of Arab Fund aid to Jordan in 1998 was in the form of loans with just 1 per cent of Arab Fund assistance in the form of direct grants. Loans have been approved for projects of technical assistance to improve irrigation and address social inequality and unemployment, as well as supporting the construction of the Mujib Dam in the southern Jordan valley. With better relations with Kuwait restored following King Hussein's death, the Kuwait Fund for Arab Economic Development (KFAED) is once again likely to be a major source for development assistance.

Another significant contributor of loan aid to Jordan is the Islamic Development Bank, which according to figures from Jordan's Ministry of Planning, extended loan aid of some 18.6 per cent of the total the country received in 1998. The main part of this assistance will be directed to carrying out development projects including infra-structure projects in poorer districts. This package is comprised of a US$ 43.5 million loan and a US$ 650,000 grant. This loan aid is particularly important given the principles governing interest (*riba*) employed by the IDB; because of Shari'a prohibitions on interest charges, compatible modes of financing are employed in the activities of the bank with only a service fee being charged on loans. The service fee, according to the IDB, represents nothing more than the actual expense of the loan incurred by the Bank rather than any profit from the loans which the Bank might generate under other circumstances. As such these loans from the IDB in 1998 were extended for projects to improve provision of healthcare infra-structure in Jordan, the education sector, and to 'finance part of the civil works required for the implementation of the Social Productivity

Programme' (Ministry of Planning, 1998, p. 11). All this demon-
strates that Jordan's important position in the Arab and Islamic world
has played a significant part in its ability to attract this assistance and
support for recovery, political divisions not withstanding.

All this high profile international economic activity aimed at underpinning a major player in the MEPP helped King Hussein to point up
the benefits of peace with Israel to his people who largely remained
sceptical. He had also hoped that Jordanian businessmen would profit
from bilateral trade with Israel and from access to the Palestinian
market, which had been virtually captive to Israeli exporters. In this he
was disappointed. Despite the opening of transport links and some
Israeli investment in establishing textile companies taking advantage
of Jordan's skilled and cheap work force, bilateral trade has remained
at a trickle. Israeli exports to Jordan were worth $9m compared with
only $5m imports from the Kingdom (Israel Ministry of Foreign
Affairs, website, October 1998). Nor was Jordan able to take advantage of opportunities on the West Bank. According to the Jordanian
Trade Association (JTA), 1998 exports to the PNA territories only
amounted to $25m (Jordan Times, 10 March 1999, p. 3). The
president of the JTA was quoted as believing that $300m would be a
reasonable target for such exports, representing only 10 per cent of the
value of Israeli trade with the PNA. Certainly the new relationship
with Israel has had no discernible positive impact on Jordan's traditional trading patterns and the popular perception remains – in this
case supported by economic data – that there is little or no 'peace
dividend' discernible as a reward for the pursuit of domestically
unpopular policies. This perception was coloured by more or less
perpetual stalemate in the MEPP once the Likud government of
Binyamin Netanyahu came to power in Israel in 1996.

The issue of water remained on the political agenda as a
significant bone of contention affecting Jordan's ability to engage in
economic recovery. An attempt to increase its share of hydro-
resources with Israel had been a major motivating factor in
propelling King Hussein into formal peace with Israel. In the past
Jordan had complained bitterly of Israel's attempt to divert waters
from the River Yarmouk, which in turn feeds the River Jordan, into
its own territory. Accordingly when Israel and Jordan signed the
Treaty of Peace on October 26,1994, an attempt to settle water
issues via Article Six was a significant provision amongst the thirty
articles and five annexes which formed the text of peace between the

two countries. As Lukacs notes, the treaty states that the two countries 'agreed upon a water-sharing regime in the Jordan and Yarmuk rivers and Israel undertook to provide Jordan with 1.8 mcm a year from the northern part of the country. In addition the two countries pledged to co-operate to alleviate the water shortage in the region by developing existing and new water resources, by preventing contamination of water resources, and by minimising water wastage' (Lukacs, 1997, p. 195).

While the agreement did not satisfy Jordan's basic grievance that Israel had engaged in the theft of another country's national resources by diverting source waters, it did outline new rules for future co-operation. Nevertheless, in 1999 significant political dispute threatened to erupt as Jordan complained that Israel was reneging on a commitment to supply water to Jordan because of poor winter rains over the border. Arguing that this violated the terms of the Peace Treaty and its Annexes, Jordan was able to pressurise Israel to comply with its own commitments and begin to supply the bulk of the promised water. This was a particularly important achievement as Jordan suffered a severe drought in 1999, which has led to a sharp fall in its agricultural production.

During the three years following the Oslo Agreement and the Israel-Jordan Peace Treaty, the Washington based IFIs expressed considerable public satisfaction at the progress of Jordan's structural adjustment programme. The main economic achievements of successive governments since 1993 and the main parameters of the modern economy are discussed below, but to the average Jordanian economic success, however presented in Washington or Amman, was neither tangible nor credible. As the former Crown Prince, Hassan bin Talal remarked to the then British Foreign Secretary, Malcolm Rifkind, in March 1997: 'The fundamentals of the economy are sound but you can't eat fundamentals'. This was in the wake of serious riots on the 1989 pattern in August 1996, sparked off by a World Bank prescribed removal of subsidies on basic foodstuffs in August 1996 at a time when more people than ever were under the official poverty line and disparities in wealth distribution appeared to be growing. Popular disillusionment with the government's economic policies were undoubtedly compounded by frustration over continued stalemate in the MEPP and opposition to a policy of confrontation with Iraq, perceived to be neither in the Kingdom's political nor commercial interests but in those of the US and other western allies.

## TOWARDS ECONOMIC RECOVERY

As the previous sections have explained the basic parameters of Jordan's economy have not fundamentally changed in recent years. The constraints are familiar: a lack of natural resources – the growing disparity between the availability of water and the demands of a rapidly growing population and expanding economy being the most serious, and a shortage of exploitable minerals, the absence of oil and inadequate productive land. Owen and Pamuk defined two main characteristics of the Jordanian economy in the 1980s which still apply with some force today. The first is the predominance of the services sector rather than manufacturing in the economic activity of the country. The second is that although Jordan is a country without oil, it still possesses many of the elements of a rentier state owing to its continuing dependence on oil related income from the Gulf. The effects of these two factors in the 1990s remained significant to the ability of the country to engage in major economic recovery and restructuring. The large size of the service sector, for example, and the correlating decline in manufacturing and agriculture in Jordan has contributed significantly to the economic problems the country has experienced and there is, in reality, little evidence that as result of restructuring programmes this feature has changed. Government spending, then, remains dedicated to a sector of the economy associated with non-tradable goods, seriously affecting the level of revenue which the state can expect from its own economy.

Trade in goods and services has provided up to 70 per cent of GNP since the mid-70s; the services sector contributed over 60 per cent to the Kingdom's GDP. This is in part a reflection of the lack of raw materials and also the effect of the central role played by a government and administration in receipt of increasingly large amounts of aid (periodic hiccups and hiatuses always excepted), much of which they could distribute as they liked. Inevitably a high proportion is spent on public services: civil bureaucracy, the military – maintaining an army theoretically technically prepared for combat with Israel – and on the maintenance of a formidable security/intelligence apparatus, which before 'liberalisation' in 1989 was designed to quell any manifestation of political opposition against the regime. By the mid-1970s nearly half the total labour force of 360,000 were in these categories and much the same proportions apply today. However, there is emerging evidence of a recent growth in the private sector, especially with the new emphasis on the

IMF mantra of privatisation, which makes Jordan more of a genuine 'mixed economy' than was the case 20 years ago.

The rentier characteristics of the economy remain an important feature and a target for reform. As described above, the downturn in oil prices from the early 1980s on caused Jordan severe difficulties with a decline in remittances and in subsidies from the Gulf States. Structural adjustment is partly targeted at minimising such dependence and financial support from the IFIs and a broader spread of donors compensates for a reduced income from the oil producers. Obviously continued dependence on aid inflows is only intended as an interim palliative until the economy achieves self-sufficiency. But in the meanwhile familiar rentier elements still predominate. For example: the high propensity to import inflated wage rates, a tendency to inflation and high value of the currency in relation to major regional trading partners. High-wage, high-cost industry has only been able to survive with a considerable degree of protection and industrial and agricultural development has accordingly been hampered. Reduction and removal of subsidies are aimed at minimising the problems arising from protectionism – essential anyhow for meeting World Trade Organisation (WTO) criteria, for which organisation Jordan is a candidate member.

King Abdullah II has inherited an estimated US$6.8 billion in foreign debt, compelling him early in his reign to mount a major tour of western capitals in an attempt to lobby for debt reductions. He and government ministers have stated that the economy is his top priority. The Minister of Finance told one of the co-authors in May 1999 that a 50 per cent reduction in bilateral debt would be a major factor in sustained economic recovery. Abdullah duly made his pitch during his tour and is clearly counting on friendly western leaders to help the smooth transition to 'the new Jordan' through sustained economic support. As one palace official was quoted, 'Debt forgiveness is a political decision, not an economic one. We hope there is enough goodwill to help Jordan'. He emphasised the importance of doing so as debt servicing alone is currently costing the country $400 million annually (Faraj, 1999, p. 1).

The new King has directed his government to speed up IMF-agreed economic adjustment programmes by further liberalising the economy as a means to lift the country out of recession, marked by serious unemployment with levels unofficially cited at as much as 27 per cent and widespread poverty. These attempts reflect the down-turn in fortunes at the end of the 1990s with negative growth reported for 1998 and an acknowledgement by Prime Minister Rawabdeh that, 'We have passed from a period of slow growth to a period of recession. Every single person can feel stagnation', and concluding that, 'the solution is not easy nor will it come in a short while and it might take difficult measures' (Jordan Times, March 1999).

The government has outlined four major areas in its strategy for recovery, including improving the investment environment to create more jobs, improving the performance of the public sector, treating poverty and unemployment and continuing a policy of openness to the outside world. But this model of economic liberalisation does not tackle the core features of an underdeveloped economy which have held it back. Policies aimed at debt forgiveness and broadbased strategies to liberalise the economic environment of the country are commendable as far as they go. But they are not enough to tackle major problems such as the depressed agricultural sector, the continuing drain on the economy of the service sector, the high levels of poverty and unemployment. And, of course, eliminating corruption in high places. Finding a cohesive answer to these issues remains the greatest challenge to the new King's reign. He has recognised this, knowing that the economic security of the country will guarantee the political stability of the Kingdom.

# Chapter 4

## INTERNATIONAL RELATIONS

### INTRODUCTION

Any assessment of Jordan's foreign policy over the past fifty years has to take into account a number of factors. International relations between the rulers of this Kingdom and other state actors in the regional and global context have been shaped by two basic imperatives. The first has been the supremacy of the monarchy in the foreign policy-making process in Jordan. King Hussein, in particular, was personally respons-ible for the traditional balancing act which Jordan undertook while he was on the throne. Although instinctively pro-Western and anti-radical, yet anxious to avoid isolation within the Arab world, the conduct of international relations in Jordan has born all the hall-marks of a ruler who achieved short-lived periods of equilibrium between these two polar opposites in the balancing act. A saga of constant calculation (often miscalculation), the story of Jordan's international relations is as much about the ebb and flow in the fortunes of its late King and his strong emotional pulls rather than sober economic or strategic calculations in the foreign policy making process. It is perhaps too soon to determine if the new King will also call all the shots in deciding his country's foreign policies. Early indicators are that this is likely to be the case.

While it is important to acknowledge the role of the King in the foreign policy making process a second set of fundamental issues must be addressed when outlining processes of policy making in the Kingdom. These bear directly on the wider issues of foreign policy and international relations, which any nation state in the contemporary global order must take into account. They include, according to al-Khazendar: the maintenance of 'Jordan's internal stability, and external security; to mobilise and utilise foreign aid and resources for economic and social development; to deal with the Palestinian issue through Jordan; to strengthen Jordan's position within the region; and to affirm the unity of Arab security through joint Arab action' (al-Khazendar, 1997, p. 17).

Some of the issues outlined above would fall under any foreign policy remit in other states in the region. Other considerations, such as foreign aid and the Palestinian question, however, have led to the unique shaping of foreign policy in the kingdom. All of these will be examined in the course of this chapter by an analysis of the relationships Jordan has built up with a variety of other actors in both the regional and international context. The importance of foreign aid on Jordan's economy cannot be understood without examining the country's relations with the 'monarchies' of the Gulf Arab states, as well as the influence of the United States of America, Europe and Japan. In addition, Jordan's foreign policy needs to be interpreted within the context of the Palestinian-Israeli conflict. Even the conclusion of a peace treaty between Jordan and Israel in 1994, which has ushered in a new era of foreign relations for the country, has not altered the importance of the resolution of the Middle East Peace Process and the Palestinian-Israeli conflict as a major foreign policy objective.

As our initial comments indicated, the foreign policy making process in Jordan is *sui generis* in a number of respects, primarily because of the way in which it became the personal property of the late King Hussein. This phenomenon does not have its roots in any formal constitutional provision. Rather it reflects the historical circumstances whereby a young and inexperienced monarch was catapulted into a regional cauldron of inter-nation tension and crisis. In addition, the King's monopoly on the foreign policy function needs to be understood in the context of the late 1950s. Hussein, barely out of his teens, in order to retain his leadership of the kingdom (and indeed the kingdom itself), ordered a complete crackdown on domestic political life and thus moved towards autocratic control of all policy-making functions in government. At that time the young King could barely trust those within his own government after he had discovered that among their number some had plotted to oust him from power. After this experience political expediency and sheer survival became entrenched in the realm of foreign policy making. As Mutawi points out, 'Since Jordan has always been heavily dependent on other nations, the survival of the Kingdom is closely tied to foreign affairs' (Mutawi, 1987, p. 8). It is hardly surprising therefore that the King did not care to delegate the responsibility for making foreign policy decisions.

The constitutional basis for the formulation of foreign policy is, however, worth examining. Firstly, the constitution of 1952 stipulates that the government of Jordan (Council of Ministers) has respons- ibility for 'administering all affairs of the State, internal and external'. Thus a clearly defined foreign policy function is outlined. Neverthe- less, even the 1921 Constitution promotes the ultimate authority of the King in the foreign policy-making process by declaring in both Articles 31 and 48 that 'The King ratifies the laws and promulgates them ... The Prime Minister and Ministers shall sign the decisions taken by the Council of Ministers, which shall be submitted to the King for ratification in all cases required under the present Constitution ...' (Constitution of the Hashemite Kingdom of Jordan, articles 31 and 48). Thus, while in theory this constitution promotes all the usual legislative mechanisms and authority for the foreign policy making function, it also sanctions and upholds the authority of the King to alter, endorse or withhold endorsement of any legislation relating to this process that he so chooses.

Over the past fifty years this constitutional base to the foreign policy-making process and, more significantly, its actual practice, has encouraged a decline in either Parliament or government initiating foreign policy directives. It has lent a legal basis to the King's pre-dominance and allowed the monarch to legitimise the limit of the extent of his ministers' influence with regard to this important function of government policy. This has in turn tended to determine the foreign policy agenda, an agenda which, at certain historical junctures, had more to do with the balance of power in the sphere of influence around the King than the national interest of a small and intrinsically insignificant kingdom in the Middle East. At other times, the striking of a chord between King and citizens on a foreign policy issue, as with the Gulf Crisis in 1990, has been tellingly employed to maintain internal stability and the survival of the Hashemites as rulers in the region.

Now that we have identified the monarch as pivotal in the modalities of foreign policy making we should examine the process in action and the institutions that support the King in this particular function. Under King Hussein foreign policy was influenced by a coterie of close advisers and functionaries of the Royal Court. While it is true that formally the royal court is the primary political and administrative link between the monarch, government, armed forces and security services, historically it has played a more important role in government than its official position might indicate. Far from being a mere facilitator between monarch and government, the Royal Court is much more than an 'errand boy' between ruler and ruled.

As discussed in Chapter Two, authors such as Mutawi perceive the Royal Court as an institution 'as influential as the Cabinet', and others have remarked on its advisory capacity in the decision-making process undertaken by the King. Indeed, as Owen points out, the Royal Court reflects the distribution of power poignantly: 'its pattern is structured by the dictates of a system in which rulers need political servants to advise them and to carry out their orders ... in the theatre of legitimacy' (Owen, 1992, p. 62). Traditionally, it has been argued that the Royal Court has been engaged and been influential primarily in domestic affairs. But logic dictates that given the prominence of this institution to the King and his activities in the domestic sphere, the international relations of the Kingdom must also be influenced by this powerful group in a variety of ways. If, as previously acknowledged, parliament and the foreign ministry are not involved in the process of foreign policy making and the power of the court is at least on a par with the Cabinet, then the impact of this group on the monarch's decision-making regarding Jordan's position abroad should not be ignored nor underestimated. As in all 'Courts', power and influence vary with the individual standing of the senior courtiers at any one time, especially the holder of the position of Chief of the Royal Court. The extent of his influence depends entirely on the degree of his personal rapport with the King.

Within the hierarchy of the Court a number of other key posts remain more important than others, with the potential to 'bend the ear' of the King over matters relating to foreign affairs and international relations. Here again the personal standing of the individuals concerned is decisive. But as mentioned above the most prominent post remains that of Chief of the Royal Court, often wielding more political clout than the Prime Minister. The first incumbent of the post under Abdullah II, Abdelkarim Kabariti, is widely perceived as 'more influential' than the Prime Minister Abdelraouf al-Rawabdeh. He was described by Badareen as expecting to play a significant role in foreign policy, influencing the new King in determining what direction regional relationships, in particular, should head (al-Quds al-Arabi, March 4, 1999).

Other positions within the court of the King also remain significant in relation to the formulation of foreign policy, such as the King's advisers on military, economic and national security issues – as always depending on who the incumbent happens to be. The role of the economic adviser, for example, can be significant because of the dependence on external funds for the survival of the country and the maintenance of political stability. However he is probably not so influential as the Governor of the Central Bank (or some Ministers of

Finance) who act as the 'interface' with the donor community. Similarly the head of the National Security Council, a member of the Royal Family, is important as a cousin of the King's and because of his role as liaison with the Chief of the Jordanian general intelligence department – GID (*Mukhabaraat*).

It is this small group of individuals that advises the King and allows him the opportunity to sound out particular strategies or programmes before the fait accompli of policy is presented before the Jordanian people, via the Council of Ministers and Parliament, for rubber stamping. It is, therefore, this small group along with their King who have some responsibility for both the successes and failures of Jordanian policy abroad. As such tension has often existed, for example, between the Prime Minister and the Royal Court, where under the late King influence depended more on personality rather than position. For example, when Kabariti was Prime Minister in 1996 he had the royal ear to a much greater extent than the Chief of the Royal Court Marwan Qassim. By the same token we believe he is much more influential than Prime Minister Rawabdeh with Abdullah II.

Yet power and influence at this level of decision-making, whether it concerned foreign policy or domestic politics, is all relative. Since at least 1989 the late King tended to rely less and less on his advisers – ministerial or courtly. He was known to be impatient with views he did not share and even the most senior long-serving old friends hesitated to give him advice they knew would be unwelcome. By 1993 one high ranking foreign diplomat observed that the King's advisers were 'little more than sycophantic courtiers reminiscent of the court of King Henry VIII rather than a modern twentieth century monarchy'. Moreover, the King when genuinely seeking advice turned to individuals on the basis of what they could contribute to a particular topic. Long after his disgrace in 1989 on charges of corruption Zeid Rifai, for example, although holding no formal position, greatly influenced the late King on Syria.

What then, are the objectives behind the policies formed by this small elite surrounding the King? What factors have guided the foreign relations of this country? Mutawi suggests the most fundamental of goals: plainly put, 'survival', he declares, 'is the principal foreign policy objective to which all ... aims are subject' (Mutawi, 1987, p. 25). Is Mutawi trite or profound in identifying this primary feature of Jordanian foreign policy and what does he mean by it? On the one hand it appears obvious to declare that 'survival' is the central plank of Jordanian foreign policy calculations. Surely, in this respect, Jordan is no different from neighbouring states in the region? All regimes exist to survive and from a realist perspective of international relations foreign policy is about the durability of the nation state.

On the other hand, the import of the assertion that survival has everything to do with Jordan's foreign policy objectives rests on an acceptance of its uniquely vulnerable position within the Middle East. As we have previously explained Jordan is regarded as a 'pivot' in the region, bordering as it does radical Arab states, Gulf monarchies and Israel. Its unique quality is that more than half of Jordan's population comes from or is directly descended from a population from outside its own borders and a people who are still struggling for self-determination and independence. Jordan is also a country with a built-in dependency on the developed world, initially on Britain who carried much of the country's financial burdens up to the 1950s, and more recently the wider international community, notably the United States, the European Union and the Washington based IFIs whose collective financial assistance keeps the Kingdom afloat. Moreover unlike any other Arab country outside the Gulf, Jordan has the West, or more precisely, the United States as its military supporter of last resort. It is against this background that Mutawi's survival argument has validity.

In striving for the survival of the Kingdom and with the integral role of the monarch at its heart King Hussein pursued a number of foreign policy options throughout his decades on the throne. Buffeted by the winds of regional politics, his blueprint for survival was to attempt to chart a narrow course between the radical Arab world and the West. In so doing he was influenced by the historical legacies of the Hashemite family and the continuing need to create a nation with a distinct identity. The threats he faced were from radical Arab nationalism, as represented first by Nasser's Egypt and subsequently by his Syrian neighbours, and the pressures his neighbours exerted by playing the nationalist card in Jordanian domestic politics. Through open and covert diplomacy, attempts at regional brokerage, avoidance of isolation and dependence on the revenues of others, Jordan and its leader steered a path of survival against the strongest odds. What remains remarkable about these successes – and survival has to be counted a success – is that, for the large part, Jordan has not had recourse to force.

Apart from the ill-fated and unavoidable participation in the 1967 war and the crushing of the Palestinians in 1970–71 ( simultaneously expelling a Syrian incursion), military action was generally discarded as an option from an early stage, both as a tool of foreign policy and as a means of ensuring internal control. This was perhaps less a matter of choice than a realistic assessment of Jordanian capabilities. Rather the King pursued a policy of active diplomacy within the region, establishing himself as a broker for peace on the international stage and at the same time exploiting the pursuit of external aims as a means of reducing internal pressures. His success was such that at the time of his funeral the enduring memory of the late King was as an international rather than regional leader.

BETWEEN IRAQ AND A HARD PLACE: THE RADICAL ARAB STATES

A number of factors can be identified as significant in understanding why Jordan has pursued a variety of strategies in its foreign relations with her neighbours, the radical Ba'athist states of Iraq and Syria. What is clear is that despite an instinctive tilt to the West, no particular ideological line has governed the relations which King Hussein pursued with his radical neighbours. Nor have historical disputes, such as the Iraqi overthrow of their Hashemite monarchy in the 1958, hindered the promotion of periods of warm Iraqi-Jordanian relations. Rather, economic and trade considerations have played a large part in Jordanian calculations, along with the persistent desire to be all things to all men within the region as well as on the international stage. Finally, King Hussein's policy towards Iraq and Syria had a distinctly dual nature about it, with one side promoted over the other as circumstances changed. One cannot, therefore, ever point to a period when Jordanian-Iraqi-Syrian relations were in harmony, enjoying equal treatment in the palaces of Amman, Baghdad and Damascus. This was mostly due (since the 1960s) to the endemic rivalry which bedevilled the relationship between the two branches of the Ba'ath party holding power in both Baghdad and Damascus rather than as the result of any Jordanian action – or lack of it. In essence the policies that King Hussein pursued in relation to his radical neighbours was not necessarily always in the national interest, but rather reflected the balancing act which the King performed in terms of regime survival, management of the Palestinian issue and promotion of Jordanian economy and trade.

In its relationship with Iraq Jordan has enjoyed an erratic record, entering into alliances, pacts and commitments which have, on occasion, seemed to have steered the country onto a collision course with the rest of the region and beyond. The nature of this relationship has not always been clear. In the late 1950s and 1960s Jordan was extremely wary of extending a hand of friendship to a state which had deposed King Hussein's cousin the Hashemite King Faisal, destroyed the monarchy and installed a one-party regime led, after some upheaval, by Saddam Hussein. The radicalism of Arab socialism as epitomised by the Ba'ath in Iraq had proved a dangerous and destabilising factor in the late 1950s, as the young King Hussein struggled to assert his authority over the country and suppress the forces of Arab socialism and radical nationalism in his own backyard.

Accordingly, throughout the 1960s and 1970s Iraq and Jordan were largely hostile to each other as the Hashemite monarchy struggled for survival in the era of Arab radicalism, spearheaded by states like Iraq. In addition, Iraqi support for Palestinian resistance and fedayeen activities against Israel, and Iraq's threat in 1970 to use its own expeditionary forces in Jordan in support of the PLO on the eve of civil conflict only served to exacerbate the already poor relations between the two countries. When the fighting started, the fact that Iraq failed to deploy its forces alongside the PLO indicated that there had been a belated change of heart in Baghdad with the PLO being told that 'pitting the Iraqi state against the Jordanian one was unacceptable' (Sayigh, 1997, p. 264–5). This *volte-face* was welcomed in Amman, particularly as it coincided with more threatening action on Jordan's northern border where Syrian troops invaded in support of the PLO in their conflict with Jordanian forces, as the first military engagements with the Palestinians took place.

Syria's decision to cut diplomatic ties with Jordan in 1971 in support of the PLO only served further to demonstrate the growing distrust between these two states at a time when relations with Syria's rival Iraq warmed. While it would be unfair to say that from 1970 onwards a special relationship between the two countries emerged, contacts notice-ably thickened between them throughout the 1980s. The area in which the new relationship would prosper was initially in trade and aid. Aid-dependent Jordan, eager to expand its trading base and develop its ports and roads, encouraged the financial overtures which emanated from Baghdad throughout this period. While relations with Syria also improved after 1973, the lure of a profitable commercial relationship with Iraq involving cheap oil, a valuable export market and preferential trade deals including free trade areas proved irresistible for the

Jordanian monarch. He believed that a strong economic relationship with oil-rich Baghdad would help secure the Hashemite monarchy and bolster it against any Syrian expansionist tendencies on its northern border. Iraqi support for Jordan on the Palestinian issue helped Jordan promote its policies on the regional stage against an increasingly concerted PLO-Syrian front.

By 1980 the relationship with Baghdad was cemented even further as Jordan announced its support for Iraq in its war against Iran and trade agreements increased as Iraq geared up its economy for conflict with its Persian neighbours. Indeed, as detailed in chapter three, by 1981 as a result of various 'trade and aid protocols' Jordan's exports to Iraq increased from $42.3m (1979) to $186.8 m. (Day, 1993, p. 564). This came at a point when Jordanian-Syrian relations had deteriorated further as both countries sought to destabilise the other by supporting opposition forces in each other's states. Jordan's ill-disguised role in supporting Syrian Islamists of the Muslim Brotherhood mount a challenge to Asad's regime in 1979 and 1980 backfired as Asad crushed his opponents and then turned his army back to the border with Jordan. By December that year the Arab press was reporting Syrian jet attacks on alleged Muslim Brother bases in northern Jordan. Saudi mediation prevented a full-scale ground offensive between the two countries. In addition, it was believed that Syria's hostility to Iraq had also been a significant factor in its actions against Jordan, 'that another objective of the military moves was to stop attempts by Amman and Baghdad to isolate Syria' (New York Times, December 21, 1980).

Yet even the threat of Syrian troops on Jordan's northern border did not prevent the King from taking his country into a closer embrace with Iraq throughout the rest of the 1980s. In this respect, Jordan was not alone neither within the region, nor internationally in seeking to benefit from the Iraq–Iran conflict. The Gulf monarchies supported Iraq along with major backing from Western powers such as the United States of America, Britain and France. In this respect, Jordan's support only differed by degree. Similarly, the effects on Jordan's economy also differed in extent becoming progressively locked into the Iraqi market and increasingly dependent on Saddam Hussein's prosecution of his campaign against Iran.

As described in the previous chapter, the economic benefits to Jordan in siding with Iraq during the decade long war against Iran were significant, turning, for example, the hitherto underdeveloped port town of Aqaba on Jordan's Red Sea coast line into Iraq's major access point. Transit trade, income from import duties and two way trade between Iraq and its Jordanian neighbour expanded with considerable financial benefit to Jordan. Indeed, by the end of the decade the great majority of ships docking in Jordanian Aqaba bore goods not for Jordan itself but neighbouring Iraq. In addition, the Iraqi-Jordanian trading link, combined with Iraq's increasing dependence on Egyptian migrant labour, led to a massive flow of human cargo between the three states. The free-entry policy offered by Iraq to Egyptian labour meant that by the end of the decade some hundreds of thousands of Egyptians had traversed through Jordan to work in Baghdad and other Iraqi towns and cities. Additionally, as the war progressed and Iraqi spending exceeded its resources, the Jordanian economy became further entwined with its neighbour's because of the export of goods to Iraq against lines of credit extended by Baghdad. This was at a time when the economy began to overheat and the inevitability of economic restructuring could no longer be ignored.

The end of the war meant further economic setback for Jordan as Iraq was compelled to address its own impecunious situation and the decline in external funding which had flowed from Gulf states throughout the war. Indeed, the Gulf Arab states suffering from depressed oil prices now began to demand evidence of a commitment to start the repayment of their loans. While King Hussein gave every appearance of continuing the close relationship between Amman and Baghdad, other foreign policy preoccupations, including the Palestinian Intifada and (since 1985) a gradualist *rapprochement* with Syria, forced him to take stock of the direction in which the hitherto close relationship with Iraq was taking him.

On the positive side the Iraqi relationship had allowed Jordan to profit financially and diplomatically – brokering better relations between Iraq and Egypt and playing a major role in the creation in 1989 of the Arab Co-operation Council (Jordan, Iraq, Egypt and North Yemen) within the region. On the negative side, however, it meant that even if King Hussein had wanted to distance himself from Saddam Hussein's invasion of Kuwait in August 1990, his earlier mis-calculations made it hard for him to do so.

Proximity, however, should not be interpreted as the basis for the *de facto* federation of Jordan and Iraq during the Gulf crisis that some authors have talked about (Baram, 1994, p. 136). While it is true that Jordan gave all the appearances of supporting Iraq (rather than Iraqi war aims), the explanation of this lies in the entangled relationship between the two which has been outlined above. As described in chapter two, another important factor was the unqualified popular support extended to Iraq in the streets of Jordan. As King Hussein persevered with his efforts to pursue an 'Arab solution to an Arab problem', his regional colleagues and much of the international community quickly showed their disapproval of Jordanian support of Iraq.

The effect of UN sanctions on Iraq (including a naval blockade of Aqaba) and the knock-on effect on Jordan, plus the damage caused by the retaliation of regional countries against the Kingdom is outlined in detail in the previous chapter. It is worth repeating briefly that the cumulative effect was to seriously jeopardise the country's economic recovery. According to the economist Fahd Fanek, 'Jordan's compliance with the UN sanctions against Iraq ... hurt Amman five times as much as Baghdad' (Middle East Mirror, 29.8.1990, p. 3). Although this was a trifle fanciful it was being reported by September 1990 that Jordan faced economic collapse unless it received substantial assistance. This was needed to ameliorate the combined effects of sanctions, loss of trade with Iraq and the Gulf, the significant costs of absorbing a new flood of refugees, the curtailing of worker's remittances and the end of Gulf aid and cheap oil.

Despite these setbacks King Hussein appeared determined to 'keep the door' open with Baghdad throughout the war and refused to oppose Saddam Hussein. The rest of the world perceived this stance as sheer miscalculation as Jordan was stripped of Arab Gulf and inter-national support. Yet the way in which Jordan, surprisingly quickly, recovered its prestige and rebuilt relations, in particular with the United States, might be held to demonstrate that the King successfully played a long game to emerge relatively unscathed in terms of his own international standing. But we wonder. It is more probable that the King's speedy rehabilitation was due to the urgent need Washington had for a reliable (and familiar) partner to help push forward the peace process to take advantage of a new situation post-Desert Storm. And the Americans had expectations that the King could be 'turned' and persauded that it would be to his advantage to work against Saddam. We suspect that these US calculations are nearer the mark in explaining the King's international comeback than the success of any long-term strategy King Hussein had in mind when opposing the forcible expulsion of the Iraqis from Kuwait.

As for the King, he met US blandishments to return to the 'fold' more than halfway. He had not enjoyed international isolation and had been particularly wounded by attacks on him from a western media which had previously tended to extol his courage as 'the Plucky Little King'. Epithets such as 'King Rat' (coined by a British tabloid) and the withdrawal of an invitation to preside over a military parade at the Royal Military College at Sandhurst (where he had been a student) were particularly hurtful. In truth the King began to realise that his ambivalence over Iraq's attack on Kuwait had been harmful to his kingdom (his rhetoric at the time not withstanding), but he remained unrepentant. He never ceased to defend his conduct by pointing out that the strength of popular support for Saddam had left him no room for manoeuvre during the Gulf crisis.

Relations between Jordan and Iraq since the end of the Gulf Crisis have been far from smooth. At times, such as when Saddam's two son-in-laws defected to Amman, they have been hostile. A crisis in the relationship was also caused by King Hussein's decision, as a result of US pressure, to allow one of the Iraqi exile groups to establish themselves in Amman and to broadcast anti-Saddam propaganda aimed at fomenting opposition to the Iraqi regime. Generally speaking, Jordan has tended to distance itself from Iraq and concentrate on other spheres of foreign policy – in particular the MEPP.

Nevertheless, the commercial relationship remains important – oil supplies resumed in 1991 (with the blessing of the UN) as a means of servicing the Iraqi debt with Amman. The Jordanian manufacturing industry is still intent on recovering lost markets in Iraq through trade deals as part of the oil protocol, which enables Jordanian companies to export products to Iraq not covered by the sanctions regime. At the same time some senior politicians in Jordan, including the then Prime Minister Abdelkarim Kabariti, urged the King to distance himself further from Baghdad, principally to seek *rapprochement* with the Gulf States of Saudi Arabia and Kuwait.

But the King's declining health in the latter part of the 1990s hindered him pursuing a consistent policy on Iraq. He concentrated on maintaining a major role for Jordan in the MEPP culminating in a treaty of peace with Israel, thus securing the financial assistance of major international players like the United States, the European Union and Japan. However, he was always aware that US financial and military assistance was as dependent on a policy of at least hostile neutrality towards Baghdad as it was on playing a positive role in the peace process. He was also aware that confrontation with Iraq did not play well with his people. Public opinion (as elsewhere in most of the Arab world) opposed sanctions as punishing the Iraqi people and not influencing the regime. It was also widely felt that an anti-Iraqi posture was in accordance with a US agenda – one which advocated a policy of double standards: an eagerness to confront Baghdad and impoverish the Iraqis by all available means and an unwillingness to put pressure on an obdurate Israeli government which was failing to deliver on peace. King Abdullah II will face a similar dilemma on Iraq. He too will need to keep in with Washington, not only as a major source of financial support but also in order to avoid alienating domestic opinion at an early stage in his reign.

On Syria, King Hussein's policy of low maintenance of contacts with Iraq also led to further softening of relations between King Hussein and Hafez al-Asad, as both men faced up to problems with ill-health and the succession question in their own domestic arenas. Certainly, it can be said on the eve of the King's death that relations between Jordan and Syria, the Palestinian issue notwithstanding, had improved considerably. His successor King Abdullah II visited Syria in April 1999, symbolising his determination to maintain good relations with a hitherto estranged neighbour.

## MEETING OF THE MONARCHS: DYNASTIC RIVALRIES

The maintenance of monarchical systems of government in an area dominated by radical regimes is one of the chief factors which have cemented Jordanian-Saudi Arabian relations together for so long. In particular this relationship is often only explicable by the common thread of monarchy pushing otherwise natural rivals together in a region of populist nationalist regimes. The historical legacy of the Jordanian-Saudi dimension reflects the tension and conflict which occurred between these two families in the 1920s. At that time the Saudi's succeeded in ousting the Hashemites from their family seat in the Hijaz and usurped their position as custodians of the Holy places (Abu Nowar, 1989, p. 144).

While it is true that throughout the 1950s and 1960s the Jordanians pursued a foreign policy which laid great store on a strong relationship with Saudi Arabia, this is often explicable by the old Arab saying 'my enemy's enemy is my friend'. Targeted by the Arab radical regimes as anachronistic, imperialist leaning and unrepresentative the leaders of Jordan and Saudi Arabia found solace with support for each other at those times when the future of their dynasties looked precarious. Yet the support each could offer the other was never based on parity of esteem or resources. Indeed, the balance of power in this relationship was always firmly tilted in favour of the moneyed hands of Saudi Arabia.

King Hussein, fully cognisant of his weaker position, constantly strove to exploit the financial benefits which he hoped might accrue to oil poor, labour-rich Jordan. This relationship, according to Nevo, is based on five factors: 'the nature of the respective regimes and societies; their weight in the inter-Arab system; the asymmetry of these relations; the influence of Egypt and the impact of both the Palestinian question and Israeli-Arab relations' (Nevo, 1994, p. 106).

Nevo's factors are useful in some respects but they are not fully relevant to modern circumstances. The role of Egypt in determining the relationship between the two countries, for example, was historically specific to the threat posed by Nasser and Nasserism rather than Egypt itself, as to render it as invalid in assessing the state of play since his demise. In addition, the appearance of similarities in the nature of Jordanian and Saudi Arabian regimes and societies is largely superficial and says more about strategies for legitimising rule than the coincidence of culture and society between Hashemite Jordan and Wahabi Saudi.

The role of religion, for example, in both countries, might upon first examination appear similar. Indeed Nevo believes that 'religious fervour' is a feature characterising, to a greater or lesser degree, both Jordanian and Saudi society and that it has been a significant factor, along with 'anti-communism' in explaining commonality in the relationship between the two (Nevo, 1994, p. 107). Here Nevo is wrong. The nature and role of religion in both societies is radically different. Saudi Arabia claims to be an Islamic state, Jordan on the other hand does not. Jordan's rulers enhance their legitimacy through reference to their lineage to the Prophet Mohammed, but the political philosophy of the state is western constitutional in origin. Moreover the role of religion in everyday life is not comparable. Jordan tolerates the practice of other faiths and does not officially discriminate between its citizens on the basis of religion. In Saudi Arabia, however, citizens are not free to practice any faith other than Islam and a coercive arm of the state, the *mutawa* (religious police), rigorously maintains a strict interpretation of Muslim code. At face value there are similarities which could be said to demonstrate that the religious basis of both societies have much in common but this would be a superficial assessment. In reality religion and more specifically Islam has been a constant source of tension in the Saudi-Jordanian axis as both regimes compete to claim and enhance legitimacy through custodianship of Islam's holy places.

Indeed, it might be argued that Jordan has far more in common with the other Kingdoms or Emirates of the Gulf than Saudi Arabia: Kuwait, Bahrain, Qatar, UAE and Oman. All five plus Jordan have a background of a strong British connection, much more so than is true of Saudi Arabia. Jordan was the first to gain full independence, with Kuwait following in 1961 and the rest ten years later. British influence had been particularly strong in the development of bureaucracies, civil legal structures, financial institutions and especially military and security institutions. The individual armies depended mainly on British equipment in their early years and Oman and Kuwait still have sizeable British Army Loan Service teams in an advisory capacity. All the military forces maintain close links with the UK defence establishment, sending personnel to Sandhurst and to Military Staff colleges. The Omanis and Jordanians conduct joint training with British units. Oman, like Jordan, was for a long period dependent on the services of British seconded and contract officers. There is considerable cross-fertilisation between armed forces especially, again, between Jordan and Oman, and there were intimations in the late 1990s of further cementing military and political links – perhaps by treaty of association – between Jordan and the GCC monarchies.

The Gulf Arab states are largely monarchical and accordingly have more in common with Jordan and its (mostly) Western alignment than with radical Arab states and despite the more advanced nature of the Hashemite Kingdom's constitutional liberalisation. The Gulf Arab states have had experiments in participatory politics on a stop-go basis with the Bahraini national assembly suspended almost since its foundation, and Kuwait's parliament similarly closed down for long periods. Oman and Qatar have followed Kuwait in moving cautiously towards opening up their political systems to greater participation but are a long way behind Jordan in experiencing the same popular pressure for liberalisation.

Given the absence of dynastic rivalries, much common background and similar international alignment it is not surprising that these bi-lateral relationships have generally been cordial if, in the case of Qatar and Bahrain, unsubstantial. All five Gulf Arab states are markets for Jordanian agricultural exports. Kuwait, and to a lesser extent the UAE were, up to the late 1980s, generous to Jordan with their subsidies to a front line state in the Arab-Israeli dispute. Kuwait was an intermittent supplier of cheap oil which was an important boost to Jordan's economy. All except Oman, where rigid immigration policy has prevailed, were and remain important destinations for Jordanian/ Palestinian migrant workers. Kuwait, up to the 1990–91 – was the home of some 350,000 Jordanian passport holders who, in turn, were responsible for sending back over US$1 billion per annum worth of remittances.

The present Queen of Jordan (Rania) was born in Kuwait. Her Palestinian parents had lived there since the 1950s. The presence of such a large community caused problems for both countries. The Jordanian press, especially Palestinian journalists, tended to criticise Kuwait for undervaluing and exploiting their Jordanian/Palestinian guest workers. They were not allowed constitutional rights or allowed to own property and the Kuwaitis (and other Gulf Arab regimes) were stigmatised as reactionary and oppressive. Senior Kuwaiti personalities, especially parliamentarians and its press used to retaliate, poking fun at King Hussein and his 'sham democracy'.

Jordan's ambivalence during the Gulf crisis, perceived by Kuwait as outright support for Saddam, put a severe strain on the relationship between these two states and damaged post-war relations for the most part of the 1990s. Indeed, Kuwait for its part remained hostile to the country until the death of King Hussein in 1999, refusing to allow the return of Jordanian migrant workers to their homes, businesses and jobs in Kuwait. Some 300,000 workers had either been expelled or not allowed to return in 1990–91. The other Gulf states, with the exception of Saudi Arabia whose relations with Jordan remained notably cool, gradually mended fences with Jordan post-crisis. Jordanian-Omani relations remained largely unaffected by the Gulf Crisis both during 1990–91 and its aftermath. King Hussein enjoyed something of a special relationship with his Omani counterpart, Sultan Qaboos.

With the accession of King Abdullah II, even Kuwait has pointedly warmed up the link with Amman. King Abdullah II's proposal to visit Kuwait made early in his reign was welcomed by the Kuwaitis and put the seal on a new relationship with the Gulf state. The Jordanian Embassy has re-opened in Kuwait and it is likely that Jordanian workers will once again be welcome in the country. Given that the level of worker's remittances from the Gulf are already back to the pre-war level, it is apparent that Jordanians have found work in other Gulf countries besides Kuwait. In addition, Jordanian produced goods are now back into Gulf markets and the status quo of pre-1990 has largely been restored. The Jordanians have high hopes of financial assistance from the Gulf states to help economic recovery and were heartened by the UAE depositing funds with the Jordan Central Bank as a mark of support following the accession of King Abdullah II to the throne in 1999.

## FOREIGN POLICY FOR CONFLICT AND FOR PEACE

Until 1993, for Jordan, the seeming intractable nature of the Arab-Israeli conflict had significant implications for the country's foreign policy. It should be remembered from the outset that not only was the conflict a major foreign affairs issue, but was inextricably tied to the domestic environment as the majority of population is of Palestinian origin. Thus, while an awareness of the Palestinian dimension of the conflict is essential for understanding Jordan's foreign policy objectives, it has been discussed in detail elsewhere in this book. Accordingly the following section will focus on the wider aspects of the Arab-Israeli conflict and its impact on the Kingdom's external relations.

Firstly, it is important to note that in some respects the very birth of the country was tied into one dimension or another to the Arab-Israeli dispute. The politics of conflict have always affected the ways in which Jordan's monarchs have developed relations with other states in the region. The relationship with the Zionist movement and later the government of Israel illustrates this point. For King Abdullah I and his grandson Hussein the fighting that broke out between Israel and the Arabs in 1948 altered the nature of relations between these two neighbouring states forever. While there is considerable evidence to suggest that before 1948 there was co-operation (Shlaim, 1990), the war of 1948 ended any prospects for a formal peace between these two states for many decades. The continuation of the conflict, combined with the radical politics of Arab nationalism, compelled King Hussein to throw in his lot with Egypt and Syria in 1967 with disastrous consequences for Jordan.

The need for Jordan to align itself to the Arab position in the conflict with Israel was for many years a constant factor colouring most (if not all) aspects of Jordan's foreign policy. By endorsing the

Arab position, Jordan's own political stability at home was endangered. This was most clearly illustrated during the 1967 Six Day War when King Hussein was, against his better judgement, pushed into military battle with Israel, goaded by Nasser to prove his pan-Arab credentials. Thus, a policy which did nothing to serve Jordan's national interest was pursued because of the inescapable pressures of the wider Arab arena and their effect on Jordanian domestic opinion.

In addition, throughout the 1970s and 1980s the Arab-Israeli conflict decisively influenced the role that Jordan attempted to carve for itself both within and outside the region. There were episodes in the country's history where the King appeared to veer between one opinion and another in terms of commitment to the Arab position on Israel and on the use of the military option in the dispute. Over the years, the Jordanian position on the conflict began to shift perceptibly and the Americans were quick to identify King Hussein as a potential ally in the diplomatic efforts to bring peace to the Middle East. Yet, there remained an important question to be asked, why would Jordan break Arab ranks and make peace with Israel?

The answer of course is multi-faceted and inevitably links in to the Palestinian issue. In addition, any calculation of peace-making by King Hussein would have taken into consideration a variety of other factors, including the legacy of Egypt's cold peace with Israel and its isolation within the Arab world following the signing of the Camp David Peace Treaty. Throughout the 1980s Arab unity on the conflict with Israel figured prominently on the regional agenda and Jordan's position was under constant assessment, calculation and strategic evaluation in the royal circles of Amman. Although King Hussein attempted to pursue a policy of (often highly secret) peace-making contacts with Israel separate from the PLO and the Palestinians in the latter half of the decade, the Arab international community was ultimately able to goad Jordan back into the fold before Arab ranks were further split. Thus, the Fez summit of 1982 ended Jordanian hopes that the Reagan Plan would deliver a 'confederate' solution with Jordanian primacy in a structured Hashemite-Palestinian relationship.

Although the King sporadically attempted to pursue his own path and ignore majority Arab sentiment, he felt obliged by the mid-1980s to yield to regional pressure and accept a common Arab consensus. When necessary the PLO were able to play the Arab card against Jordan and any attempt to negotiate a separate peace with Israel was hindered by widespread sympathy for the Palestinian cause and suspicion of any plan which hinted at expansionist tendencies in the Jordanian camp. So strong was Arab solidarity on this issue that at the Arab summit in Algiers in June 1988 Jordan faced reproach for its attempt to undermine the power of PLO in the West Bank and the Gaza Strip during the first months of the Palestinian uprising (or Intifada). There is certainly enough evidence to suggest that this public rebuke and continuing hostility in the Arab world to Jordan's claim to the West Bank played a significant part in the decision announced a month later by King Hussein to abandon Jordan's claim and disengage from the West Bank.

With the advantage of hindsight one might argue that the decision to revoke the claim to the West Bank was ultimately beneficial for Jordan and allowed it the freedom to negotiate peace with Israel on its own terms rather than the Palestinian's. At the time, however, the decision was not viewed in this way, and it was seen as the direct result of the strength of Arab influence on Jordanian foreign policy. Moreover, with major financial backers like Saudi Arabia refusing to channel aid for the Palestinians via the Jordanians, the threat of jeopardising the Jordanian-Saudi axis was too great a sacrifice for King Hussein to face for the sake of continuing to carry the Palestinian burden.

If the 1980s highlighted the Arab dimension to Jordan's pursuit of peace and appropriate strategies for survival, the 1990s witnessed an entirely new phenomenon. There was a remarkable aspect to Jordanian policy for conflict resolution in the period from 1991 to October 1994 (when Jordan signed the peace treaty with Israel at the Araba/Arava border crossing). This was King Hussein's skill in exploiting an unfavourable situation and managing to outflank much of the rest of the Arab world with such panache, which ultimately brought a peaceful resolution to the Israeli-Jordanian track within the wider dispute.

One early indication that King Hussein was willing to break ranks and go his own way had come as far back as 1985, when despite Arab disquiet Jordan resumed diplomatic relations with Egypt and set about bringing Mubarak's government back to the Arab fold. King Hussein had recognised Egypt's potential support as an important ally in the peace camp. And it was King Hussein's ability to use the peace process as a way of restoring relations with the USA through his willingness to act as a 'moderating influence' which was really remarkable about this period. No doubt their knowledge of a history of covert dialogue with Israel also encouraged the Americans to believe that the time was ripe to encourage Jordan's role as broker for peace in the region. And they were certainly generous in their (financial and military) blandishments to encourage the King to stick his neck out for peace.

Israel's agreement to permit a Jordanian-Palestinian delegation at the Madrid Conference of October 1991 was just one way in which Jordan could act as a 'bridge builder' between two deeply distrustful sides. No doubt a history of undercover diplomacy and good cross-border (military to military) relations reassured hawkish elements within the Israeli defence and political establishment. At the same time the PLO believed that Jordan would faithfully discharge its responsibilities to act as an 'umbrella' for the Palestinian delegation during the negotiations; after all Jordanian claims to speak for the Palestinians had been formally renounced they could more comfortably sit on the same side of the conference table as equal partners.

The usual major sticking points which had stalled the Madrid process from 1992 onwards were in the end circumvented by highly secret talks in Norway between the Israelis and an alternative PLO delegation. These negotiations, which were successfully concealed from the other participants at Madrid, culminated in what was known as 'the Declaration of Principles' (DOP). In effect, this was a blueprint (or 'roadmap') for a peace agreement between the two sides. King Hussein was taken completely by surprise by the outcome of the Oslo talks (he had tended to dismiss hints dropped by Arafat that something was about to happen). He hesitated before giving the DOP his endorsement and support. But he felt he had to – even if he believed that the agreement was far from ideal – so as to avoid being left behind in what he believed was a gathering momentum towards a comprehensive peace settlement.

He could now go for a bilateral deal with Israel with the respectable fig leaf of being able to follow an example set by the Palestinian leadership, thus avoiding the inevitable slur from the usual critics that he was breaking Arab ranks. This was perhaps less of a worry than in the past as the Arab posture was affected by the end of the Gulf crisis and the process of realignment which took place within the Arab world vis-à-vis the West. This shift, plus the end of the Cold War eclipsing Russian (no longer the Soviet Union) influence, allowed room for further manoeuvre on the Arab-Israel dispute.

From King Hussein's perspective, peace with Israel was seen as a way in which he could enhance the status of his country in the regional theatre, setting an example for other less accommodating Arab states to follow. At the time he believed that the Syrians were nearing an agreement and was anxious not to be beaten to the draw by Damascus. Moreover, the economic dividend that King Hussein believed would accrue to his country as a result of making peace with Israel was a powerful motivator. The King relished the prospect of aid from states like America, Japan and the Europeans as support for a peacemaker. They had previously made it clear that they would be generous with their finance and with debt forgiveness or rescheduling. And he believed that there would be benefits from harmonising the Jordanian, Israeli and Palestinian markets, which would enhance the process of economic restructuring already underway in the kingdom.

The additional possibilities of a boost to tourist income from open borders, the benefits of technical co-operation, the attracting of external private investment into Jordan and establishing Amman as a regional business centre were exciting. Balanced against the loss of the Iraqi market, the knock-on effect of sanctions and the decline in aid from the Gulf states, the economic spin-off from peace with Israel must have been very alluring. The weight of these considerations are summarised by Lukacs when he states: 'From a Jordanian perspective the reasons for agreeing to sign ... the peace treaty on October 26, 1994, were related to the Israel-PLO Declaration of Principles and to Jordan's economic predicament' (Lukacs, 1997, p. 191). This historic act of peacemaking also set the seal on Jordan's reconciliation with its natural allies and sponsors in the West, wiping the slate clean in the aftermath of the Gulf crisis.

## TILTING AT WINDMILLS: JORDAN AND THE WEST

As earlier observations in this chapter and in the historical outline attest, Jordan's relationship with the West has always presented the Kingdom with difficulties in terms of its position in the region as an Arab/Muslim state. At times, the dilemmas inherent in the dual nature of foreign policy-making has resulted in the appearance of a rather Janus-faced attitude in the Hashemite Royal court to both Arab neighbours and Western states. Despite occasional episodes of schizophrenia Jordan has become and has remained one of the region's most pro-Western states. Periods of tension and disagreement with the West have been relatively short-lived and are explicable by reference to the regional political framework rather than any ideological shift within the Kingdom.

In the past it has been said that Jordan enjoyed a special relationship with Britain and that King Hussein had a particular affection for the country. Certainly it is true that in a romanticised and nostalgic sense there is a special tie between the Hashemites and the British. Anyone who believed otherwise would certainly have been convinced by the extraordinary turnout by members of the British establishment and ordinary citizens from every walk of life at the late King's memorial service in July 1999 at St. Pauls Cathedral in London. Many of the Hashemite family have been at least partly educated at British schools and at military establishments such as Sandhurst. King Hussein's second marriage was to a British woman (Toni Gardiner – the mother of the present King), there are close links between the two royal families and of course, Britain had a vital role in the establishment of the Kingdom. Many ordinary Jordanians also had a special regard for the United Kingdom because of the close contacts between the two countries in so many spheres of activity – military, educational and commercial.

In present-day Jordan things are somewhat different. Whether the Hashemite Royal Family does or does not retain a special affection for Britain (and they probably still do), ordinary Jordanians are not sentimental about Britain and its role in the country. The old exclusive relationship has gone for good. It is not necessarily the visibility of the British presence in Amman which indicates who is the most important Western power, but the realities of Jordan's dependence on aid and who are the most generous benefactors. In this respect, the British-Jordanian relationship is better subsumed in a European one, along with, for example, France and Germany.

There are some areas of the British-Jordanian connection which are, however, still substantial and worth examining for their significance. Military co-operation between the two countries has endured and remains a cornerstone of good relations. Jordan has been a constant beneficiary of British-manufactured military hardware, most recently the subsidised purchase of Challenger battle tanks. Its forces have benefited from shared opportunities for training and the military culture (similar drill, compatible uniform and pipe bands) in Jordan reflects a British standard. In this respect the relationship is likely to continue while on other areas of British-Jordanian relations a more pan-European approach will be reflected in the way Jordan chooses to look at the British connection.

The affection for Britain in royal circles is unlikely diminish under the new monarch, given his mother's British roots and his own (fondly remembered) experiences of being educated and raised for part of his childhood in the country. While British aid is subsumed under the wider European aid programme to Jordan it constitutes 16 per cent of the total, the UK has been at the forefront of debt rescheduling and debt swap arrangements. Britain also converted US $80 million worth of loans into grants to mark the success of King Hussein's peacemaking efforts. The UK is also a major trading partner and has substantial investment in the manufacturing and tourist sectors.

Jordan's relationship with The United States of America is on a different level altogether. It does not reflect any of the old misty-eyed nostalgia of the British-Jordanian dimension. Following King Hussein's decision in 1956 to remove Glubb Pasha and other British officers from the Jordanian army, which led to the ending of the British subsidy, the US stepped into the breach. This was part of American strategy – somewhat hesitantly as far as Jordan was concerned – to head off the spread of communism within the Middle East. Over the next decades Washington became a significant supporter and financial backer of the Hashemite kingdom.

Since 1953 the American government has offered aid assistance of up to $2 billion to Jordan – an indication of the level of importance America attaches to the Hashemite kingdom. Yet, in terms of total expenditure in the region US assistance to Jordan is not overgenerous as compared with support for Egypt (and Israel). The bulk of funding has been comparatively recent and closely related to encouraging the peace process in the 1990s. According to Satloff, America did not in the first instance willingly step into the big brother role vacated by Britain in 1957. Indeed, as Satloff asserts: 'the creation of that strategic relationship was far from assured; America was reluctant to assume Britain's responsibility for propping up an enterprise that was viewed as unviable' (Satloff, 1996, p. 117). Ironically, despite the change in Godfathers it was British troops, and not American, which came to Jordan's assistance in 1958 (following the overthrow of the Hashemites in Baghdad).

As we have just mentioned, the tentative beginnings of this association should be put within the wider context of America's policy of containing the Soviet and communist threat within the Middle East theatre, a strategy articulated in the Eisenhower Doctrine of 1957. The sheer tenacity of the Hashemite monarchy (contrary to most observer's expectations) during an era of regional turmoil from the late 1950s to late 1960s convinced the US that this was a regime worth backing. Washington therefore helped to provide enough financial assistance to keep the country in the black. This was an important contribution towards maintaining the pro-western sympathies of its ruling elite.

King Hussein, himself having secured aid from America, found himself increasingly dependent on Arab assistance and remittances from Jordanian workers in Gulf states during the 1970s. Mutually beneficial though it was, the relationship with the US had a different character to the British-Jordanian bond and in many respects neither side hankered for such an association. The US government was happy to keep the Jordanians on side so long as the Kingdom did nothing to undermine US policy objectives with other Arab states in the region including, of course, Israel. This attitude was illustrated in the 1980s during the Reagan administration when despite an initial attempt to bring Jordan into the peace process under the terms of the Reagan Plan the Hashemites were sacrificed in US support for Israel's invasion of Lebanon in 1982. This was combined with reluctance in the US Congress to increase financial and military aid to Jordan, mostly because of effective pressure from the pro-Israel lobby.

While it is true that in the past no 'special relationship' developed along the lines of the US-Iran (during the Shah's time) or US-Israel ties, Jordan has increasingly played an important part in US policy objectives in the Middle East. In the 1990s there was increasing evidence of the attention that the US State Department and National Security Council Middle East specialists were giving to the role that Jordan might play in support of America's pursuit of a peace process. In addition the US was soliciting Jordanian support for a strategy to confront and contain Saddam Hussein.

The King was quick to capitalise on his support for this aspect of US policy and from the mid-1990s onwards assumed the mantle of 'bridge builder' between Israel and the rest of the Arab world, as well as continuing to act as a 'moderating influence' in general. He also displayed a more belligerent attitude towards Iraq. His readiness to support US policy produced the rewards he had anticipated and is graphically illustrated in terms of US assistance to Jordan. USAID funding to Jordan, for example, jumped from $7.2 million in 1996 to $140 million in 1998. In June 1997 President Clinton announced a bonus payment of $100 million to Jordan and a further $100 million for the next 4 years in recognition of King Hussein's role in pushing the peace process forward. In addition, American recognition of Jordan's pivotal role in the region and its quest for stability through economic restructuring has resulted in debt forgiveness, soft loans and loan guarantees, military assistance and equipment and so on totalling $271.6 million in 1999 alone (USAID paper on US Assistance to Jordan, 1998, p. 1).

The death of King Hussein, 'Prophet of Peace', in early 1999 did nothing to diminish American support for Jordan. Indeed, the US government quickly assembled a formidable aid package to further bolster support to the new King Abdullah II and encouraged other governments to follow suit. To what extent these factors point to a 'special relationship' between Jordan and the United State is debatable. Nevertheless, Jordan is considerably beholden to the United States. At present, the financial support that the American government can lend through direct aid or its influence in international forum such as the IMF or World Bank cannot currently be matched by other players, although the European Union and Japan are also a significant source of financial support. At the same time direct financing from the richer Arab countries has declined whilst American and other Western assistance has increased.

The political implications of the US-Jordanian relationship are important. While it is true that Jordan is anyhow traditionally pro-Western and for its own reasons inching towards political liberalisation, one need only look at Egypt to realise the full significance of any degree of dependence on such a powerful international player as America. It will be interesting to see to what extent the new King takes account of the adage: 'He who pays the piper calls the tune.' Should Jordan grow increasingly dependent on American assistance, independence in foreign policy and the Jordanian national interest could become the subject of increasing sacrifice. While historically Jordan and Saudi Arabia have experienced setbacks in their relations, by and large Jordanian dependence on Saudi did not come at the expense of political and regional independence. In a sense Jordan borrowed within the family. But its relationship with America runs the risk of alienating it from the Arab arena in the service of American national interest and foreign policy objectives in the Middle East. This would not matter if there were a strong mutuality of interest between Amman and Washington. But in reality there are important areas of regional politics – such as how to deal with Iraq – in which Jordan may feel obliged to bow to the will of its wealthy patron, despite the damage it may suffer. Perhaps more happily for the sake of an independent Jordanian foreign policy other important donors, notably the Europeans and the Japanese, do not seek a political quid pro quo for their support.

If we accept that the United States has been Jordan's protector of last resort since 1958, then it follows that there can only be limited freedom of movement for Hashemite Jordan within this relationship. In these circumstances the most that Jordan's foreign policy makers can strive for is to optimise correlation of national interests and minimise the differences. For example, on the issue of relations with Israel – until 1994 – there was inevitably a considerable difference between American and Jordanian national interests. King Hussein was tasked with selling a highly unpopular peace deal at home; as one journalist, Robert Fisk, reported: 'there was no dancing in the streets of Amman' when Jordan's king signed up to peace with Israel.

Popular disquiet at the new relationship with Israel has failed to be diminished by the (as yet unrealised) promise of 'peace dividends'. National unity has been eroded, thus setting back, in turn, as the late King forced through an unpopular policy of normalisation, the limited steps towards political liberalisation which had been evident in the country. Coincidence of interest has largely been lacking as America has continued to encourage Jordan into a warm peace with its neighbour, while at the same time Jordan has suffered from a lack of Israeli reciprocity. The attempted murder of an Islamist leader by Israeli agents in Amman in the autumn of 1997 highlighted what little regard the Netanyahu government seemed to have for Jordanian efforts on the peace front. Yet despite the difficulties, the King seemed to accept that American support or assistance was the 'only game in town'. As Garfinkle has remarked: 'The weakness of Western Europe was such that although its attitude to the Arab-Israeli conflict better pleased the king, it could not substitute for the United States either to protect Jordan *in extremis* or to pressure Israel effectively in the context of a diplomatic process' (Garfinkle, 1994, p. 292).

Jordan is not really just a client state totally dependent on the West. The considerations of obligation to powerful sponsors have always been balanced with the demands of Arab and Muslim identity. As this chapter has described, the late King Hussein of Jordan spent the majority of his reign engaged in a delicate balancing act between the Janus-faced demands of Jordan's Western leanings and an Arab and predominantly Muslim popular base. The Jordanian establishment has always been more Western-leaning than its people a tendency based on a realisation that the survival of the state depended on an ability to survive during an era in which superpower rivalry in the Middle East was an inescapable condition and when economic independence was out of the question.

In these circumstances it was inevitable that the ruling elite pursued or maintained relationships with the West, and only raised the spectre of a closer alignment with the Soviet Union in times of crisis when it appeared that Jordanian interests were being neglected or threatened by their usual friends, knowing full well that to do so would rivet Western and especially US attention.

The end of the Cold War has removed for the moment the option of exploiting Big Power rivalry. Moreover, in the 1990s, the noose of debt, the need for aid and economic dependence has propelled Jordan further into the American-dominated Western camp. And it occurs at a time of American hegemony in the region where choice is a limited option for the Hashemites. The new monarch will benefit from American support of his kingdom and the Americans have already indicated their faith in Abdullah II and their determination to maintain stability by financially supporting the 'new Jordan' and through further commitments to military assistance and high-profile diplomatic support. The other donors and the international community as represented by the IFIs are also likely to be generous to ensure that King Abdullah gets off to a good start. The long-term implications of this are examined in our concluding chapter.

# Chapter 5

## WHITHER JORDAN?

### INTRODUCTION

The smooth transition from King Hussein to his successor Abdullah II amidst memorable scenes of genuinely popular and nation-wide grief underlined the extent to which the Hashemites have earned their legitimacy as the ruling family of Jordan. There is an enormous sense of loss but also a feeling of seamless continuity. Moreover, to anyone visiting the country at that time and since, it is striking how palpable a feeling of national pride exists at all levels of Jordanian society. The amazing (and unprecedented in the Middle East) turnout of regional and world leaders for the late King's funeral in February 1999 indicated to the ordinary Jordanian citizen the importance of King Hussein as an international figure and the widespread respect he had earned for himself and his tiny country.

The present-day legitimacy as virtually unchallenged and unquestioned head of state was a personal achievement for the former King. His grandfather, whom we should now refer to as Abdullah I, carved out Transjordan as a recognisable national entity within the borders it enjoys today. But it was Hussein, after a shaky start when at times he, his regime and his country faced extinction, who finally established the kingdom as a sovereign independent state as legitimate as any of its neighbours and 'sisterly' countries within the Arab world and indeed further afield. The Hashemites are no longer 'refugees' or 'incomers' from the Hijaz placed on shaky thrones as part of a British imperial strategy. They may have been, in another branch of the same family, the former unlamented monarchy of Iraq, which was overthrown in 1958.

But as far as Jordan is concerned, to quote Hudson: ' The question of legitimacy and identity in Jordan must be treated in the context of the rise and decline of the whole Hashemite family in modern Arab politics. And the future of the family is in turn linked to the fortunes and misfortunes of the British in the Arab east. The Western connection, in which the Americans succeeded the British, has proved to be the curse as well as the lifeline of the family' (Hudson, 1977, p. 210). Jordan has moved on since 1977 – British 'fortunes and misfortunes' hardly matter at this stage. The US relationship is still very significant as discussed in our previous chapter. But whatever the importance of the 'Western connection', the Hashemites are unchallenged as the rightful rulers of Jordan. They are accepted as such by the vast majority of the Jordanian people and by the wider international community. This is King Hussein's most important achievement and his legacy to his country and to the region.

King Abdullah II, as his father's son and as his chosen successor, is the new unchallenged monarch. There are no doubts as to his personal legitimacy and his right to rule. The unexpected nature of his arrival as King in the place of a Crown Prince who had been in waiting for thirty years surprised many including, we believe, him. But this dramatic change in a long familiar scenario of succession has not been opposed and is widely accepted as the late King's wise (and some say only viable) choice. Had the former Crown Prince Hassan succeeded as previously expected then we suspect the end result would have been no different in terms of popular acceptance, at least in the early stages of his reign.

This is not the place to speculate in any detail on the reasons for the late King's last minute – almost last gasp – change of heir. He may have felt that his brother, the rather bookish and uncharismatic Crown Prince, just would not do as his successor. Indeed many people believe that the late King had for some time not intended his brother to succeed, but the sudden deterioration in his health forced him into hasty action. If this is the case Abdullah was probably the safest available substitute as the other possible serious contender – the King's elder son by his fourth wife, Queen Noor, Prince Hamza – at just 18, was too young to risk. We believe that had the late King enjoyed a normal life span it is probable that he would have, at some future date, arranged for Hamza to take over as Crown Prince in Hassan's place.

Abdullah had always seemed destined for a purely military career from an early age. Admittedly he was nominated Crown Prince when he was a baby. This was in accordance with the constitution (Article 28), which stipulates that the monarch's eldest son should hold this position. Presumably because of the precarious state of the Kingdom (and constant threats against the King) in the mid-sixties, and mindful of the potential difficulties should a small child have to take over, Hussein appointed Hassan, then aged 17, as Crown Prince, amending the constitution as he did so. Hassan remained in this position until the dramatic announcement shortly before his brother's death.

Abdullah was brought up by his mother – King Hussein's second and English wife. He had a traditional Hashemite upbringing with education in the UK and the US, plus the obligatory military training – all in Britain including an attachment to an army unit. He then had a purely military career in Jordan and commanded the elite Special Forces brigade. Hardly anyone, to our knowledge, ever considered him as a likely candidate for the throne. He certainly was never groomed for this responsibility. Apart from his exclusively military focus, his Arabic was weak (he usually preferred to speak English). There is little doubt that any serious contender for the highest office would have worked hard on his native language, as Abdullah has, belatedly, been obliged to do.

Whatever the reasons for King Hussein's choice of successor, the enthusiasm which has greeted the arrival of King Abdullah II is mostly a transfer of popular love and respect from the old monarch to the new. King Hussein' s aura lives on, enveloping his son and heir. It is also partly an expression of widespread popular expectation that a new epoch has arrived for Jordan. A new, young, dynamic leader, free of much of his late father's 'political baggage' (especially in terms of regional antagonisms) might, many believe, accelerate a programme of political liberalisation – initiated and then frozen if not reversed by Hussein.

As part of a popular wish for sweeping reform, many hope that the new monarch will lead a campaign against corruption in high places, tackle a faltering economy with vigour and resolve and put the rule of law and respect for human rights at the top of his agenda. In so doing Abdullah II is expected to replace the late King's former advisers now apparently guiding the new monarch with a younger, 'cleaner' set of ministers and senior officials – a new elite for an older discredited one. Several months into his reign however, although the 'organ grinder' has gone, the 'monkeys' from his father's time have been retained. Advocates of reform, although hopeful of positive progress in the domestic scene, seem less confident about loosening Jordan's dependence on external (mostly Western and predominately US) financial support, and therefore on toeing lines dictated by Western (perceived as American) priorities – MEPP and Iraq – rather than pursuing a purely Jordanian national interest.

It is a truism that the ascent of a new king is the start of a new era for Jordan after 47 years of King Hussein. At the time of his death in February 1999 most adult Jordanians could not remember any other ruler. To most people outside the Kingdom the former King was the personification of Jordan. The one was inseparable from the other. Given the change of monarch and in the knowledge that under the former regime the King ruled as well as reigned we need to explore the extent to which a different sovereign will be able to bring about the new Jordan. It is indeed a new era but is it a markedly different one?

We believe that expectations of dramatic change are at least premature, especially so within the power structure and political organisation of the Hashemite Kingdom. King Hussein may have been something of a one-man band during the last years of his rule but he remained beholden to a small circle within the ruling elite; it was family rule supported by tried and trusted cronies. His authority, however strong his personal prestige, ultimately rested on the armed forces and the intelligence apparatus. As Owen put it: 'Jordanians outside this small elite had little or no opportunity to influence policy at the national level, (Owen, 1992, p. 65). This will remain the case. As a new and inexperienced ruler it would be surprising if the influence of the King's closest advisers (presently those who served his father) was not much greater than during Hussein's last years, when they were more (often sycophantic) courtiers than sources of generally accepted advice.

Abdullah II will for some time need to feel his way and rely on the experience and guidance of the older generation of his late father's circle. But even when he has established himself it seems inevitable that any new generation of advisers will come from the same narrow segment of the traditional elite, who will also continue to fill key positions in the armed forces and intelligence structure. Jordan will be (initially at any rate) more of a genuine oligarchy than was the case during King Hussein's last authoritarian decade with the monarch sharing power with a small self-perpetuating clique and some 'junior' members of the Hashemite family aspiring to positions of power and responsibility denied them during Hussein's reign. It should be remembered that even the former Crown Prince Hassan had virtually no authority and only marginal influence during his brother's reign.

If this assessment is accurate it does not augur well for those hoping for significant reforms, especially with regard to increased democratisation or more liberalisation of the political structure of the state. The ruling establishment will not wish to surrender their power whether politically or economically. Abdullah II may have scope for fiddling at the margins and earn some popularity with the political radicals by, for example, toning down the current draconian press laws – as indeed he has promised to do. But a transfer of real power to popular forces is highly unlikely. Jordan will remain a 'monarchical democracy' for the foreseeable future with an impressive degree of liberalisation in theory but highly circumscribed in practice, as described in the preceding chapters.

In 1977 Hudson wrote that the 'legitimacy crisis in Jordan is political and not social' and described the ways in which the King had resisted demands for increased political participation and power from his nationalist, left wing opponents (see chapter two). That was the 1970s. But into the new millennium, King Abdullah II may face a different kind of crisis which will be social and economic rather than political. The new King, by placing economic recovery at the top of his agenda, may already be anticipating this possibility. The problem with this wholly admirable objective is that it depends for solution on policies for economic reform, which emanate from a protectionist elite anxious to preserve their privileged position enshrined within the status quo. They are, therefore, instinctively averse to any serious overhaul of the economy – debt-ridden and ailing though it is. We suspect therefore that revolutionary new thinking advocating genuine reform may not figure too strongly in the King's entourage.

Initially the new regime was given the benefit of the doubt by the traditional opposition, the Islamic Action Front (IAF) and its followers amongst the professional organisations and white-collar unions. However, external events such as further stalemate in the Middle East Peace Process or developments in Iraq could lead to domestic criticism of Jordan's external policies. If this is coupled with the continuing absence of a feelgood factor via the economy, pressure is likely to build once again for more popular participation in policy making through parliament, and for a more responsive government in partnership with the legislature than was the practice under King Hussein.

In such circumstances, seeds of confrontation, at present dormant, between palace and people could easily and quickly be reactivated. If that happens there is a danger that the regime would react with coercion rather than with further liberalisation and political compromise. As Hudson reminds us, traditionally, Jordan has a record (more prevalent at the time he was writing than recently) of ' reliance on the instruments of repression and coercion because of the existence of politicised elements actively opposed to the system' (Hudson, 1977, p. 210). In the 21st century these are likely to remain the Islamists, student and radicalised professional groups and Jordan's expanding poor.

Whether or not King Abdullah II remains a 'prisoner' of his present coterie of advisers (or is conscious of the need to rule with their consent), he certainly seems determined to tackle obstacles in the path of some areas of much needed reform. The King has placed the economy at the top of his agenda. The Prime Minister Abdul Raouf Rawabdeh told the Jordanian Parliament on 24 May 1999 that the country had no choice but to follow tough economic reforms to help revive the recession hit economy. (Jordan Times, 25 May 1999). Much hope is being placed in massive debt forgiveness by Jordan's major creditors. According to Finance Minister Marto, King Abdullah's first European/ US tour in May 1999 was primarily aimed at securing relief of up to half Jordan' s bilateral debt of $4 billion.

Abdullah II was received sympathetically in Western capitals and a subsequent G7 meeting called for a constructive and flexible approach to Jordanian debt. But attempts to secure this level of debt forgiveness are unlikely in global terms. Other much poorer countries may have a better case for pleading special treatment and although some relief may be forthcoming as a measure of support for the 'new Jordan', including yet more debt rescheduling, it is unlikely to be enough to put the economy to rights as the sole panacea.

Accordingly it seems inevitable that further belt tightening on the traditional IMF/ IBRD prescription will be needed. Measures include the complete removal of remaining subsidies, increased sales and other taxes, more privatisation (with the likely consequences of an increase in already high levels of unemployment), and less tariff protection for domestic industries – as one of the conditions adherent to the WTO. Jordan already has at least 30% of its people living under the official poverty benchmark and expensive 'safety net' social welfare benefits will need to be put in place if this section of the community is to escape further punishment.

The professional middle classes already feel squeezed by the restructuring programme, which they have endured for a decade. And although they seem prepared to support the government in its attempts at reform, further economic sacrifices are likely to be resented and resisted unless the government can be seen to be dealing equitably with all its citizens and make a real attempt at effective wealth redistribution. The super rich of suburban Amman live in ostentatious splendour, seemingly unscathed by financial stringency. Popular belief equates much of their wealth with unscrupulous and opportunist land speculation and corruption. From their ranks come most of the ruling clique, including some of the senior members of the present government who have large question marks against their personal integrity and whose past (all too public) misdemeanours have gone unpunished because of personal influence with the system of justice. Any reform programmes they initiate and which seem to exclude them and their cronies from sharing in the pain will lack credibility, and could once gain lead to the repetition of the food riots and other violent protests which shook the Kingdom in 1989 and 1996.

The King's apparent determination to make the economy a top priority has been welcomed in the main donor capitals and, in principle, (so far) by his people. He has also been praised for efforts to mend fences with those other Arab countries that had not enjoyed the best of relations with the Hashemite Kingdom since the Gulf crisis of 1990–91. The high turnout of Arab leaders at the late King's funeral signalled the intention of such countries as Syria, Saudi Arabia and Kuwait to start afresh with a new young monarch who they hoped had discarded his father's 'baggage' of historical regional animosities and suspicions.

In the early months of his reign Abdullah II was in almost perpetual motion visiting neighbours and others further afield, taking advantage of this new honeymoon of reconciliation and co-operation. Full diplomatic relations have been restored with Kuwait and there is new cordiality with Saudi Arabia. Most importantly the Damascus-Amman axis appears to be basked in a warmth not known for many years. Much of this is of purely psychological importance to Jordan – warm acceptance of a new King and a rejuvenated country within the greater Arab family. But there could be important practical benefits. The re-opening of the Gulf for Jordan's skilled and surplus workforce (barred from Kuwait since 1991) and unimpeded access to traditional markets in the same region could play its part in aiding the current programme of economic recovery.

As discussed in the previous chapter it is only with Iraq that there is hesitancy and uncertainty with Jordan facing contrary pressures. On the one hand there is a popular desire to restore a normal relationship with Iraq – a close neighbour and despite sanctions, Jordan's most important trading partner – while on the other hand there is strong pressure from the US government in particular to confront Iraq – including maintaining rigorous sanctions on Saddam Hussein. This policy rests on the American hope that Jordan can be used as part of an active anti-Iraqi coalition which might lead to an eventual change of regime in Baghdad. The new King, like his father (post-Gulf crisis), might well privately favour a robust posture of confrontation with the current Ba'athist dictatorship but he knows such a policy will be deeply unpopular in Jordan, not only amongst people at large, but also with the radical opposition, the larger business community and crucially amongst some influential members of the ruling elite who have benefited from extensive, surreptitious (and generally illegal) trade with Iraq in contravention of sanctions. King Abdullah II is therefore likely to remain studiously neutral in his public attitudes towards the Baghdad regime whilst discreetly encouraging efforts to get rid of Saddam. Thus he may hope to restore a normal and warm relationship with his most important neighbour which can be fostered without the risks of either alienating Washington or his own public opinion.

The King's visits further West referred to above are a recognition that a good relationship with Arab brothers notwithstanding economic salvation lies elsewhere. Jordan will remain dependent on external financial aid throughout the foreseeable future. Most of this will continue to come from the developed world, either bilaterally or through the Washington based International Financial Institutions (IFIs). As fully discussed in previous chapters, the US is likely to remain the most generous of Jordan's bilateral donors. It is sufficient to re-emphasise here that King Abdullah II will remain exceedingly cognisant of American expectations of Jordan's role within the region in return for the continuation of economic support for the Kingdom. Although non-American aid is unlikely to be directly linked to political factors there is likely to be some, if unstated, correlation between it and a donor judgement as to the effectiveness of the contribution that King Abdullah will make as a player in the peace process.

The likelihood must be that the post-Hussein Jordan will lack much of the clout enjoyed by the late King, whose sheer longevity by regional standards and close ties with the West over four decades gave him a special position to which his successor cannot hope to aspire. Neither now nor in the foreseeable future can Abdullah II expect to be more than a bit player. Jordan, by having made its peace with Israel, has lost some basic leverage. Although it remains a party to much unfinished business within the peace process, its young King has, at this early stage of his reign, little if any influence on the other main protagonists. It is doubtful if the regional 'superpowers', Egypt and Syria, will welcome intrusive participation by tiny Jordan unless it is in uncritical support of their own policies.

Despite its lack of clout commensurate with its real power Jordan will still need to try to engage itself closely and carefully if only to protect its own interests, especially with regard to the relationship with an emerging Palestinian entity. Other 'final status' and associated issues will also bear watching as being of importance to Jordan. These include the difficult problems of refugees, the status of Jerusalem and the division of scarce water supplies on the West Bank. These loose ends are of course entangled with the final shape of the territory to be controlled by the Palestinians.

Whether or not 'Palestine' eventually amounts to something approaching a sovereign state as it is understood today is as yet uncertain. Be that as it may, the Jordanian regime will still need to continue to monitor the effects of West Bank developments on public opinion within the East Bank Jordanian Palestinian community. The question of a future link between Jordan and Palestine is still highly contentious and the subject of continuous speculation in both communities. There are obvious pitfalls, adroitly avoided by King Hussein of which King Abdullah II will need to be wary, such as possible attempts by other parties – in practice likely to be Israel – to persuade Jordan to, in effect, take over the responsibility for the good behaviour of all Palestinians in a Federal or Confederate arrangement. From an Israeli perspective such an arrangement would link Amman with the Palestinian National Authority (however this may evolve) and would involve the clear control of any such political structure from Amman.

This prospect of 'Jordan as Palestine' was at times an alluring one to significant right wing elements within the Israeli political establishment in King Hussein's time. But the Israelis may now calculate that an inexperienced King Abdullah II would not be able to deliver such a convenient arrangement as they used to believe (unrealistically) King Hussein would if suitably persuaded. If only by a beguiling vision of both sides of the Jordan once again unified under the Hashemite crown.

King Hussein used to duck this issue by reference to the oft-repeated mantra that the time to consider a formal link with Palestine would be after its final emergence as an independent sovereign state. This remains the official line for the moment and is likely to do so until the nettle has to be grasped when such a union seems a viable option and/or it is formally proposed by the Palestinian leadership. The equally sensitive other side of the same coin is the question of 'Palestine as Jordan.' This is not just a semantic distinction but reflects a real concern by East Bank nationalists that the prospect of an entirely unviable Palestinian entity on the West Bank might lead to a virtual Palestinian takeover of the East. Hence these nationalists are reluctant to contemplate the granting of full civic and political rights to Palestinians domiciled in Jordan, in the fear that they might dominate parliament and other public institutions. They would also oppose more Palestinian refugees from the West Bank coming into Jordan, preferring them to return to their homeland across the river. An advocate for such hard liners, Abdul Hadi Majali, the Speaker of the National Assembly, reopened the whole controversy by calling on King Abdullah II to resist those who were trying to force him to 'adopt plans relating to the Palestinians that conflict with Jordanian national aspirations' (Al Quds Al Arabi, 5 August, 1999). This is an issue which will need sensitive handling within the Government's stated policy of protecting national unity by treating all citizens equally, irrespective of origin.

To round off this brief look into our crystal ball, it is probably safe to say that despite Jordan's 'demotion' to division two in the Peace Process League, it will continue to be supported by the West. Washington especially will continue to see it as a strategic, if minor partner, in an important region (always assuming, if only from a US perspective, that Jordanian policies are continued to be seen as helpful and in support of Western ones). We expect that the Kingdom's continued stability and economic progress (if it continues) will be held up as an example of good governance and political liberalisation worthy of further encouragement especially so in a state with a positive role still to play in resolving an old and seemingly intractable conflict. Ironically therefore (to be a touch cynical), a comprehensive peace in the region would not be in Jordan's interests, as present levels of economic support would lose much of their justification. Also, given a change of regime in Iraq and its subsequent return to the international community, Jordan would inevitably diminish in importance as a pivotal state. But that, for the moment, is not an immediate prospect.

# Select Bibliography

Abidi, H.H. 1965: *Jordan: Political study 1948–1957.* London: Asia Publishing House.

Abu-Jabareh 1993: *Economy of Peace. In Fischer, Roderik and Tuma.*

Abu-Jaber, K. 1969: *The Legislature in the Hashemite Kingdom of Jordan: a study in political development.* The Muslim World, vol. 59, pp. 220–50.

Abu-Nowar, M. 1989: *The History of the Hashemite Kingdom of Jordan. Vol. 1: The Creation and Development of Transjordan, 1920–1929.* Reading: Ithaca Press.

Abu Odeh, A. 1999: *Jordanians, Palestinians and the Hashemite Kingdom in the Middle East Peace Process.* Washington DC: USIP.

Al-Madfai, M.R. 1993: *Jordan, the United States and the Middle East Peace Process.* Cambridge: Cambridge University Press.

Allan, J.A. (ed). 1996: *Water, Peace and the Middle East: Negotiating Resources in the Jordan Basin.* London, New York: J.B. Tauris.

Amawi, A. 1992: *Democracy Dilemmas in Jordan.* Middle East Report *(MERIP).* No. 174, pp. 26–29.

Anderson, B. 1983: *Imagined Communities: Reflections on the origin and spread of nationalism.* London: Verso.

Antonius, G. 1938: *The Arab awakening.* London: Hamish Hamilton.

Aruri, N. 1972: *Jordan: A study in political development, 1921–1965.* The Hague: Martinus Nijhoff.

Ayubi, N. 1997: *Islam and democracy.* In Held, D. *et al.* (eds.)

Bailey, C. 1984: *Jordan's Palestinian Challenge 1948–1983: A Political History.* Boulder, Col.: Westview.

Bar-Joseph, U. 1987: *The best of enemies: Israel and Transjordan in the war of 1948.* London: Frank Cass.

Baram, A. 1994: *No new fertile crescent: Iraqi-Jordanian Relations, 1968–92.* In Nevo, J. and Pappe, I. (eds.)

Beblawi, H. 1990: *The Rentier State in the Arab world.* In Luciani, G. (ed.).

Bin-Talal, Hassan 1982: *Jordan's quest for peace.* Foreign Affairs, vol. 60:4, pp. 158–70.

Bin-Talal, Hassan 1984: *Palestinian self-determination: a study of the West Bank and Gaza Strip.* London: Macmillan.

Bin-Talal, Hussein 1962: *Uneasy lies the head: an autobiography.* London: Heinemann.

Bin-Talal, H. 1992: *Keynote Address, The Middle East and Democracy.* St. Andrews University: BRISMES.

Brand, L. 1994: *Jordan's Inter-Arab Relations, the political economy of alliance making.* New York: Columbia University Press.

Brand, L. 1995: *Palestinians and Jordanians: a crisis of identity.* Journal of Palestine Studies, vol. 24:4, pp. 46–61.

Brand, L. 1999: *The effects of the peace process on political liberalisation in Jordan.* Journal of Palestine Studies, vol. 28:2, pp. 52–67.

Cleveland, W.L. 1994 : *A History of the Modern Middle East.* Boulder, San Francisco & Oxford: Westview Press.

Dann, U. 1984: *Studies in the history of Transjordan, 1920–1949.* Boulder: Westview.

Dann, U. 1987: *'The Foreign Office, the Baghdad Pact and Jordan'.* Asian and African Studies, vol. 21, pp. 247–61.

Dann, U. 1989: *King Hussein and the challenge of Arab radicalism: Jordan 1955–1967.* New York: Oxford University Press.

Dann, U. 1992: *King Hussein's Strategy for Survival.* Policy Papers No. 29. The Washington Institute for Near East Studies. Washington.

Day, A.R. 1986: *East Bank/West Bank. Jordan and the Prospects for Peace.* New York: Council for Foreign Relations.

Day, A.R. 1998: *Jordan's Economy* London: Europa Middle East and North Africa, pp. 648–663.

Dearden, A. 1958: *Jordan*. London: Robert Hale.

Dessouki, A.E.H. and Aboul-Kheir, K. 1991: *The politics of vulnerability and survival: the foreign policy of Jordan*. In Korany, B. And Dessouki, A.E.H. (eds.)

De-Shazo, R. and Sutuerlin, J.W., 1994: *Reassessing the Middle Eastern 'Peace Pipeline' in the aftermath of the Gaza-Jericho Agreement*. New Orleans: University of New Orleans.

Ehteshami, A. and Murphy, E. 1996: Transformation of the corporatist states in the Middle East, *Third World Quarterly,* Vol. 17:4, pp. 753–772.

El-Droos, S.A. 1980: *The Hashemite Arab Army. 1908–1979.* Amman: The Publishing Committee.

Elmusa, S.S. 1995: *The Jordan-Israel water agreement. Journal of Palestine Studies,* vol. 24:3, pp. 63–74.

Faraj, C. 1999: King begins major tour of Western capitals today, *Jordan Times,* 8 May.

Feiler, G. 1994: *Jordan's Economy, 1970–1990*. In Nevo, J. and Pappe, I. (eds.).

Finer, S. 1970: *Comparative Government,* London: Pelican.

Gelber, Y. 1997: *Jewish-Transjordan relations*. London: Cass.

Gerner, D. 1994: *One Land, Two Peoples: The Conflict Over Palestine*. Boulder, Col.: Westview.

Glubb, J. 1948: *The story of the Arab Legion*. London: Hodder and Stoughton.

Glubb, J. 1957: *A soldier with the Arabs*. London: Hodder and Stoughton.

Graves, P.R. (ed.) 1950: *Memoirs of King Abdullah*. London: J. Cape.

Halpern, M. 1963: *The politics of social change in the Middle East*. Princeton: Princeton University Press.

Harmarneh, M., Hollis, R., and Shikaki, K., 1997: *Jordanian-Palestinian relations: Where To?, four scenarios for [he future*. London: RIIA.

Held, D. *et al.* (eds.) 1997: *Democratisation*. Cambridge: Polity Press.

Hinchcliffe, P.R.M. 1997: *Jordan: Relations with her Neighbours: Victim of War or Casualty of Peace?* Asian Affairs. London: Royal *Society* of Asian Affairs.

Hinchcliffe, P. 1999: *Interview with M. Marto*. Jordan: Amman.

Hudson, M. 1977: *Arab Politics: the Search for Legitimacy*. New Haven and London: Yale University Press.

Huntington, S. 1984: Will more countries become democratic? *Political Science Quarterly,* Summer, pp. 193–218.

Issawi, C. 1982: *An Economic History of the Middle East and North Africa*. London: Methuen Press.

IRBD, 1999: *Monthly Summary,* Washington: IRBD.

Johnston, Sir. C 1972 : *The Brink of Jordan*. London: Hamish Hamilton.

Khazendar-al, S. 1997: *Jordan and the Palestine Question, the role of Islamic and left forces in foreign policy-making*. Reading: Ithaca.

Kingston, P. 1994: *Breaking the Patterns of Mandate: Economic nationalism and state formation in Jordan, 1951–57*. In Rogan, E.L. and Tell, T. (eds.).

Kirkbride, A. 1971: *An Awakening. The Arab Campaign. 1917–1918*. Tavistock: University Press of Arabia.

Kirkbride, A. 1976: *From the Wings: Amman memoirs, 1947–1951*. London: Frank Cass.

Korany, B. And Dessouki, A.E.H. (eds.) 1991: *The Foreign policies of Arab states, the challenge of change*. Boulder Col.: Westview Press.

Lawless, R. 1998: *History of Jordan*. London: Europa, *The Middle East and North Africa 1998*. Europa Publications

Lesch, D. (ed.) 1996: *The Middle East and the United States, a historical and political reassessment*. Boulder, Col.: Westview.

Lowi, M.R. 1993: *Water and Power: The Politics of a Scarce Resource in the Jordan River Basin*. Cambridge: Cambridge University Press.

Lukacs, Y. (ed.) 1992: *The Israeli-Palestinian Conflict, A Documentary Record*. Cambridge: Cambridge University Press.

Luciani, G. (ed.). 1990: *The Arab State*. London: Routledge.

Lukacs, Y. 1997: *Israel, Jordan and the peace process*. New York: Syracuse University Press.

Lunt. J. 1989: *Hussein of Jordan: a political biography*. London: Macmillan.

Mansfield, P. 1990: *The Arabs*. London: Penguin.

Marlowe, J. 1959: *The seat of Pilate: an account of the Palestine mandate*. London: Cresset Press.

Mazur, M. 1979: *Economic Growth and Development in Jordan*. Boulder, Col.: Westview.

Maciejewski, E and Mansur, A (eds) 1996: *Jordan Strategy for Adjustment and Growth*. (Occasional Paper 136). Washington: IMR

Milton-Edwards, B. 1991: *A temporary alliance with the crown: the Islamic response in Jordan*. In Piscatori, J. (ed.).

Milton-Edwards, B. 1993: *Jordan and Facade democracy*. British Journal of Middle Eastern Studies. vol. 20:3, pp. 191–203.

Milton-Edwards, 1996: *Climate of Change in Jordan's Islamist Movement*. In Sidahmed, A.S. and Ehteshami, A. (ed.).

Monroe, E. 1961: *Britain's moment in the Middle East*. London: Chatto and Windus.

Morris, J. 1959: *The Hashemite Kings*. London: Faber and Faber.

Mutawi, S. 1987: *Jordan in the 1967 War*. Cambridge: Cambridge University Press.

Nassar, J. and Heacock, R. (eds.) 1991: *Intifada, Palestine at the Crossroads*. New York: Praeger.

Nevo, J. And Pappe, I. (eds.) 1994: *Jordan in the Middle East, the making of a pivotal state, 1948–1988*. Ilford: Frank Cass.

Nevo, J. 1996: *King Abdullah and Palestine. A Territorial Ambition*. London: Macmillan.

Nyrop, R. (ed.) 1980: *Jordan: a country study*. Washington, DC: American University Washington.

Owen, R. 1992: *State, Power and Politics in the making of the modern Middle East*. London: Routledge.

Owen, R. and Pamuk, S. 1998: *A History of Middle East Economies in the Twentieth Century*. London: I.B. Tauris.

Pappe, I. 1989: *Sir Alec Kirkbride and the making of greater Transjordan*. Asian and African Studies, vol. XXII 23, pp. 43–70.

Pfeifer, K. 1999: *How Tunisia, Morocco, Jordan and even Egypt became IMF "Success Stories" in the 1990s*. Middle East Report, Spring, pp. 23–27.

Piscatori, J. (ed.) 1991: *Islamic fundamentalisms and the Gulf crisis*. Chicago: AAAS.

Plascov, A. 1981: *The Palestinian refugees in Jordan 1958–1967*. London: Frank Cass.

Richards, A. and Waterbury, J. 1990: *A Political Economy of the Middle East, State, Class and Economic Development*. Boulder, Col.: Westview.

Rinehart, Robert. 1980: *Essay on Jordan's Historical Setting in Jordan: a Country Study*. The American University: Washington.

Robins, P. 1989: *Shedding half a Kingdom: Jordan's Dismantling of Ties with the West Bank*. British Journal of Middle Eastern Studies, vol. 16:2. pp. 162–175.

Robins, P. 1990: *Jordan's Election: A New Era?*. Middle East Report *(MERIP)*, no. 164/165. pp. 17-19.

Rogan, E.L. and Tell, T. (eds.) 1994: *Village, Steppe and State, The Social Origins of Modern Jordan*. London: British Academic Press.

Salibi, K. 1993: *The modern history of Jordan*. London: I.B. Tauris.

Satloff, R. 1994: *From Abdullah to Hussein*. New York: Oxford University Press.

Satloff, R. 1996: *The Jekyll-and-Hyde Origins of the US-Jordanian strategic relationshi*p. In Lesch, D. (ed.).

Sayigh, Y. 1997: *Armed Struggle and the Search for a state, the Palestinian National Movement, 1949–1993*. Oxford: Clarendon Press.

Shlaim, A. 1990: *The politics of partition, King Abdullah, the Zionists and Palestine, 1921–1951*. Oxford: Oxford University Press.

Sidahmed, A.S. and Ehteshami, A. (eds.) 1996: *Islamic Fundamentalism*. Boulder, Col.: Westview Press.

Smith, Charles D. 1992: *Palestine and the Arab-Israeli Conflict*. Basingstoke: Macmillan.

Starr, J.R. and Stoll, D.C. (eds.) 1988: *The Politics of Scarcity of Water in the Middle East*. Boulder, Col.: Westview Press.

Susser, A. 1990: *In through the Out Door: Jordan's Disengagement and the Middle East Peace Process*. Policy Paper No. 19. Washington: The Washington Institute.

Talhami, G. 1991: *A Symmetry of Surrogates: Jordan's and Egypt's Response to the Intifada*. In Nassar, J. and Heacock, R. (eds.).

Vatikiotis, P.J. 1967: *Politics and the military in Jordan: a study of the Arab Legion*. London: Cass.

Whitehead, L. 1992: Alternatives to Liberal Democracy: A Latin American Perspective, *Political Studies: Prospects for Democracy*, vol. XL, pp. 132–159.

Wilson, M.C. 1987: *King Abdullah, Britain and the making of Jordan*. Cambridge: Cambridge University Press.

Wilson, R. (ed.). 1991: *Politics and the economy in Jordan*. London: Routledge.

World Bank. 1987: *World Development Report*. New York: Oxford University Press.

Yapp, M.E. 1987: *The Making of the Modern Near East. 1792–1923*. London & New York: Longman.

Yapp, M.E. 1996: *The Near East Since the First World War. A History to 1995*. London & New York: Longman.

Yorke, V. 1988: *Domestic Politics and Regional Security: Jordan, Syria and Israel*. London: International Institute for Strategic Studies.

# Index